Cici

donated by
Eleanor & Howard Mack

MW01709376

# The Providence of God

# The Providence of God

## Daniel Mack

Guardian Books

Belleville, Ontario, Canada

*The Providence of God*



ISBN: 1-55306-088-1

**For more information or**
**to order additional copies, please contact:**

Daniel H. Mack
5471 St. Regis Way
Port Orange, FL 32124 USA
Tel: (904) 788-5272

Printed in Canada
by
Guardian
BOOKS

# *Dedication*

THIS IS BOTH A LETTER OF DEDICATION as well as a thank-you to all of the people who put up with me for so many years while I was writing this book.

To my awesome children, Eric and Elaine, who are both eleven (yes, they are twins) and to Ryan, who is eight. You three kept me inspired and kept me going when I said, "Oh, why bother? No body will read it anyway." Thank you, Eric, Elaine and Ryan for the encouragement during the rough times in 1998, when I really wondered what kept ME going. The three of you are very inspiring and motivating factors in my life. May you never lose your zeal or curiosity for life. Eric, you have wanted to become a preacher of the Gospel ever since you accepted Christ as your personal Savior. Never let anyone steal your dream. Elaine, you have always wanted to be a teacher, and a fine teacher you will be. You are a gorgeous young lady whom God has blessed with an incredible personality, quick wit and an insatiable desire to learn. Pass this desire on to young people around the world and it will be a far better place. To Ryan, a child with a love for animals and an unquenchable spirit. Thank you for all of your smiles through the rough times last year. Whenever you are present, there just isn't time to sit and dwell on problems. Ryan, when you were saved and baptized, it was one of the high moments of my life, and I am very glad I could be a part of it.

During the years of 1996 and 1997, I was given the opportunity to attend Grace Baptist Church, in Port Orange, Florida, the city in which I reside. For a very long time, I did not know why God wanted me to go there; I just knew that I was supposed to. The Pastor began talking about how God often works under cover, or *the providence of God.* I began to think on this long and hard until it finally hit me like a ton of bricks! That's what God does all the way through this book, and for that matter, all the way through life.

To Pastor James Guest and his lovely wife, Karla, for the incredible inspiration and Bible teaching for the two years I spent at Grace Baptist Church. I feel a close friendship with Pastor Guest and his wife. Without them, part of this book and the sequel, which is soon to follow, would not be possible.

To my wife, Teresa, a beautiful Christian who loves my children and who loves me. She was given to me by God late in the work of this book and was an incredible inspiration to me in finishing the book. Does this not show the awesome "providence of God"?

Last, but certainly not least, thanks to an incredible set of parents who have always been there when I needed them most, through the good times and the bad times, from the birth of their grandchildren to the troubles in 1998. Without you folks, I never would have gotten through that so easily.

*Love to all,*
*Dan*

# *Preface*

BEFORE YOU GET STARTED ON THIS book, let me explain how this came about. It's been nearly fifteen years since I started working on this book. It happened on a whim. I was very active in a large Baptist church in Daytona Beach, Florida. Whether you are a Baptist or Methodist, Church of God or Catholic does not really matter. What matters is whether or not you are a born-again Christian. Many people at the church wanted me to be involved in the visitation program that the church was offering on Thursday nights. "Great," I said. "I would love to do something like that." After all, it is your duty as a Christian to share the good news to others about what Christ has done for you. The problem arose when I started looking at my schedule. Sunday morning for the a.m. service, Sunday evening for the p.m. service, Tuesday morning for the men's prayer breakfast, Wednesday night Bible study and choir practice. It was close to ten at night before I got home from choir practice, then I had to get up and go to work the next morning, only to return to church again for discipleship training and visitation on Thursday night! That very quickly turns into a busy week! Something had to go. I sought after wise counsel and did much praying about the situation and finally decided that if something had to go it would be the Thursday night visitation program. But, as a new Christian, I felt bad about this. Several of my friends knew that I enjoyed writing, even if it was nothing more than putting a few thoughts down on paper, just to get them sorted out and out of my noggin! So, after a suggestion from a particularly close friend, I started putting together a few notes and going to the Bible and doing a little research and put a few things down on paper. Then I put a few more things down on paper. Soon, I had a story idea and a plot. Then there were some characters involved. After awhile, the characters had names and hence the birth of "The Providence of God." Keep in mind as you read this that this all came about in a fifteen year period. A lot happened in that time, which is probably why it took so long getting to print. Rarely did I forget the "Book," which is the name I used to save it to disk, but for months at a time, it just sat in a lonely file in the back of the hard-drive!

"Providence of God" was created in and around a dating relationship, eventually turning into marriage. Seven years later, children were born. Then came birthday parties that go along with kids being born, family vacations, job changes, moving from one house to another, and one city to another. There were the normal problems associated with family life, which took time away from the "book," and eventually in the summer of 1998, much to the protest of the children and myself, a not-so-normal problem occurred. My wife of sixteen years, who had given me three of the most wonderful children in the world, came to the realization that she no longer was in love with me and we divorced a short time later. I am not an advocate of divorce; in fact, I did everything in my power to stop this from happening. I had watched friends and relatives go through divorce and had watched what happens to the children. They are the innocent victims, caught in the middle, as are mine. I did not want this for my children or for me. But, reconciliation was not in the plan for this marriage, and it soon became apparent that she had already made future plans. (Folks, if you are reading this, please don't wait until you are thirsty to dig the well. If you are beginning to experience problems in your marriage, get help NOW, before it is too late. Avoid the big "D" at all cost.)

As I mentioned earlier, it does not matter what church you attend. There is one God with many different styles and types of Worship. The key is Worship a loving God who gave the ultimate sacrifice for His flock, that being His only son. As you read the Scriptures, you will realize that Jesus was born to die. He died for us, you and me. He paid the ultimate price so we would not have to. For that we owe Him. For that sacrifice, the very least we can do is tell others, and this is my way of "Sharing and Caring." So, follow along in a copy of God's Word, and when you finish, please, share this book with a friend or loved one. Enjoy.

*Dan*

# Chapter One

IT STARTED OUT AS THE COLDEST DAY in five years when Harvey Norman and his wife, Nancy, arose that morning. They were to depart on the first vacation they had taken in several years, and hoped to get a few things done around the house first.

During the past twenty years, Harvey has been a very successful individual in just about anything he lays his hands on, but his favorite occupation is his auto-wrecking business. Nancy, his wife of ten years has been the perfect housewife, better than any man could ask for. Deep down in his heart, he was very much in love with Nancy, even if sometimes he did not show it. Nancy continued to be the Christian, submissive wife, like she always had.

Harvey was packing some last minute clothing articles in his suitcase when he heard a mild "thump" come from the front of the house.

"That sounds like the newspaper making its morning

arrival," he said more to himself than his wife. When Harvey checked the indoor-outdoor thermometer, he found a spread he had not seen in a very long time. But, in the third week in January when living in northern New York, anything is possible. When Harvey came back in from retrieving the "Ogdensburg Post," he was chilled to the bone and looked like an abominable snowman. It took several minutes to find the newspaper; several minutes of excruciatingly cold winter time temperatures. Harvey was outraged when he came back in the house.

"As many times as I have called and written letters to that newspaper you would think they would learn! They ought to know when they throw it against the house at this temperature, it will bounce. I should build a net for it to fall into!" It all came out in what seemed like one breath, simultaneous with the slamming of the front door. "Maybe then I would not have to search the snowdrifts!"

"Is it cold out, Hon?" Nancy asked with a very sarcastic grin.

"Only if you call 32 degrees below zero with about a 20MPH wind blowing out of the north cold!"

Harvey began to unthaw his fingers a little by doing some simple finger exercises. Little did he know he would not have to deal with the cold weather for very much longer.

It was six a.m. when the last of the bags were packed. Harvey was just getting the garage door opened and the car started when Nancy came out with the last of her bags, mostly activities for her, ready for the long ride ahead.

"Well, Harv, that's the last of it. The house is all closed up and we, my dear, are ready for some sun and fun!" Nancy said with a look in her eyes that Harvey had not seen in a long, long time.

"Let's get on the road and maybe we can stop for breakfast by the time we make Syracuse. That's about three and a half to four hours down the road, it'll be about half past nine by then," Harvey said as he backed the Oldsmobile out of the driveway.

"Do you think we could stop at "Milli's Diner" in North Syracuse? The roads should be plowed, and besides...." Nancy paused for effect and gave her husband an innocent look out of the corner of her eye. He knew she was up to something anytime he saw it. It was a look that seemed to say, *"Oh, honey please don't go into an eruption. I know it bugs you when I plan an occasion without letting you in on it."*

"What's so special about 'Milli's,'" he asked. "Or is it not the restaurant you are interested in?"

At least five minutes passed before she said anything. He thought she had not heard him, or at least, had not wanted to.

For the last several years it had been quite a rocky road for the Normans. From the day they were married Harvey had made many promises to Nancy. The biggest promise and probably the one Nancy wanted most was to have her husband home more. His excuse was standard. As soon as they have life the way it should be. That was his stock answer. Now, they had it all; a very large home in an exclusive area of Ogdensburg, New York, two brand new expensive cars, (one luxury and one sport) and most of all respect from everyone in town. Anyone could walk into town and mention Harvey Norman and nothing but praise would come from their mouth. Still, even with the cars, the home, and all the respect any man could ask for there was always something lacking. Nancy could not pinpoint what it was; all she could do was speculate on a few things. She had an idea the he wanted to fly airplanes. Every time a jet would make a low pass (or even a puddle jumper) over their house, his gaze would fixate on it until it dropped from view. *All this and he still wants more.* It was her standard thought. Nancy also thought he wanted a boat, but was not real sure, and was actually afraid to ask, knowing it was rather "off-the-wall." Anytime the television would advertise something that had anything to do with boats he would lose his concentration on whatever it was he was doing.

Several minutes had gone by when Nancy answered his question. He had almost forgotten what he asked. "There is supposed to be someone there I have not seen in a while. Sorry, I guess I pre-arranged it before checking with you first," she said rather non-caring.

"Yea, you did but that's all right. I had nothing on the planning books for breakfast anyway. Besides, we are officially on vacation."

The next two and a half hours dragged for both of them. Nancy could not figure out what Harvey was thinking and Harvey could not imagine who was at the diner. They would both have to find out upon arrival.

# Chapter Two

THEY WERE ALMOST AT THE CENTRAL Square interchange before either of them spoke. "Hon, the least you should do is give me a hint as to who we are meeting? The suspense is about to kill me!" Harvey had desperation in his voice.

"Well, the only thing I can do is tell you it has a lot to do with your future. The woman's name is Kelly McGraw; I went to college with her. Right now she is living in the Daytona area and is just up here for a visit. Personally, if I were going to visit this part of the country, I would do it during a different time of the…." Nancy was cut off mid-sentence.

"So, what does that have to do with my future?" Harvey asked, rather inquisitively.

"Well, I guess I let that part slip out. You will have to wait till we get there. It should only be another ten minutes." One of Harvey's biggest pet peeves is when his wife starts to tell him something then makes him wait.

"Nancy Marie, you KNOW what it does to my boiling point when you do not finish something!" She had two indications of his growing anger. One was obvious; his face was turning beat red. The second indication was only obvious to her. The only time he ever used her middle name was when he was about to lose his temper.

"When are you gonna learn to either tell me all or just shut up!!" He knew as soon as he said it he should not have. But, ego would not let him turn back now. He was angry to the point where it could be seen in his eyes. Nancy wished she had never said anything.

* * *

They arrived at the restaurant right on schedule at 9:30 a.m. It was exactly three and one half hours from the time they had left the house. As they walked inside, Nancy looked around for her friend, Kelly. She was no where to be found so they just sat down.

"So, Nancy, where is this person that is supposed to bring a new bright spot on my horizons?" If there had been a contest for sarcasm at that particular moment, Harvey would have won first prize easily!

"Harv, I did not mean it like that. All I said was...." She was cut off by a young female voice.

"Hey, Nancy!" If her friend was trying to remain inconspicuous, she failed miserably, but in the timing department she had first prize. Milli's diner was by no means crowded, but every one that was present turned to see who got excited. Nancy and her friend met in the middle of the dining room and threw their arms around each other.

They made their way over to where Harvey was seated, then made the formal introduction. As soon as Harvey saw Kelley his whole demeanor changed. He was looking face to face with a tall, natural blonde with deep blue eyes that seemed endless. Her features were perfectly proportioned, and she was just as nice and friendly, as she was beautiful. "Harvey, this is one of my best friends, Kelly McGraw. She and I were sorority sisters in college. Kelly is now the Administrative Director and Head Guidance Counselor at a very well-known, Aviation oriented university in Daytona Beach."

As soon as the word "aviation" was mentioned Harvey's ears seemed to stand straight up. It was as though nothing else existed in the room for a few moments. He had even forgotten the little quarrel he and Nancy had just before reaching the restaurant. All was not totally forgotten though. Harv still had his big ego to think about. "So, what does a well-known, aviation-oriented university have to do with me?" he said, again very sarcastically.

"Well, Harv, it's just a premonition, or better known to you as a silly idea that I had. I have been wrong a lot in my life but in the number of years we have been married, I have learned to read you like a book. Every time a jet or even small plane flies over you will stare at it and seemingly study it. I may be off on my idea, but I think more than anything you would like to be flying airplanes. I called Kelley to meet us to possibly talk to you about it."

Harvey was getting red in the face again. "If there are any decisions to be made about my life, I would like very much to be the one to make them! If I need any outside help, which I doubt I will, I will ask for it!!!" He said, very egotistically.

Having been in many dining rooms in his life and knowing his own temper, he had learned to keep his voice down to a mild roar. But, it was loud enough so everyone in the establishment could hear it. The waitresses were beginning to wonder if there was going to be a brawl on their hands.

"Please, let's not have a family quarrel just because of my presence," said Kelley. "It's really not that important. Being the prominent businessman that you are, you probably would not be interested in something like that anyway."

Harvey realized now, even though they had just met, that she did know something about him. "How did you find out about that? Don't you live in Florida?" he asked. Curiosity had set in. He also realized, but thought better of mentioning it, that she was one truly sharp gal. She had calmed his temper down and cooled him off with one easy dose of verbal medication. He was now on the subject of her and where she lived.

"Why, yes, I do live in Florida but I am just in the Syracuse area visiting a few buddies. But, back to your question, your wonderful wife has bragged on you so much in her last few letters that I almost feel I know you. How large is your auto-wrecking facility in Ogdensburg?" Kelly asked, still trying to calm his unsettled nerves.

"It's covering about ten acres at present, but I would like to expand some." Harv still could not get over how sharp she was. He had all but forgotten about getting mad at Nancy and was sneaking a wink in every now and then. Nancy's foot was running up and down Harv's leg under the table in acknowledgment.

"Funny you should mention that, I know of a place right in Daytona that is up for foreclosure. You should check into it while you are there," she said, now totally stirring his interest.

"Yes, I may do that, but, I am quite firmly rooted in upstate New York. To pack up and leave now would be quite a chore."

"Well, Mr. Norman, from what Nancy has been writing in her letter, you have a very respectable background in the business world. Having businesses spread across the country is nothing unusual with today's travel. Please do not mis-understand me, Mr. Norman, I am not trying to talk you into anything. There are golden opportunities that have come along in the past that I would regret having missed, had I not been a little bit flexible."

Harvey Norman had absorbed every word. His brain was in high gear.

"Thank you Kelly, for that information, I really do appreciate it."

Nancy and Harvey finished their breakfast. Harvey was stuffed with eggs and bacon with toast and coffee. Nancy had her favorite, French Toast with pure maple syrup, just the way she liked it. After Kelly had left, Nancy excused herself from the table for a stop at the restroom. Harvey sat alone in the booth for several minutes reflecting on his thoughts. *I wish she would let me make my own decisions when it comes to my future. Maybe*

*I was too hard on her. It would be nice to get out of that cold. Those winters are getting too severe and lasting longer and longer. I wish things could be different at home. Aviation university. I wonder what that is all about. Nancy did not deserve the treatment I gave her a few minutes ago. Oh well, in a few hours she'll forget all about it.*

When Nancy got back from the restroom she saw her husband with the most solemn look on his face. "Harv, what's wrong, you look like you are, well.... (She did not quite know how to tell him how he really looked. He just looked at her. He knew how he looked) ...like you are about ready to cry."

"You are once again being ridiculous! I have not cried in years and I do not intend to start now!" He stole one quick glance out the window, then slid across the cool leather bench seat and stood up. "Are you almost ready to leave or do you need more time?" He said to his wife.

"Now I know something is wrong. You actually asked if I was ready without dragging me out with you. Are you going to tell me or keep me waiting?"

"No, really, I'm fine, just a little sleepy is all. C'mon let's make tracks, we still have a long way to go." Harvey offered Nancy his hand for assistance in exiting the booth, but she was almost on her feet when the offer came. She grabbed the keys from him so she could get into the car. Harvey asked his wife if she would start the car and get the heat running.

As the Norman family pulled out onto the "on" ramp of Interstate 81 South, the ramp was covered with powdered snow so deep it was impossible to see the road markings. Harvey could only rely on experience as to where the lane markings were. Harvey was wishing, and cussing under his breath, that the state of New York would get off their butt and plow the roads. It sure wasn't very safe to be traveling on. For many years Nancy had been working on her husband to stop cussing, especially around her parents. Her father, before his retirement, and eventual passing, was pastor of a small, non-denominational, Christian Church. Her mother, still living, is an extremely hard-working woman. As busy as they were they loved to entertain guests for dinner and summer barbecues, mostly just people from their church. Harvey and Nancy met at one of those church parties. Nancy was already at the party; after all it was her parents that were hosting it. Harvey, however, happened to show up in a purely coincidental sort of way. On the way home from a particularly busy day in the city of Watertown, New York, his car began acting up. Nothing serious at first, just an occasional burp or belch. But, as he got closer and closer to Ogdensburg it got worse. He was down to forty miles an hour and it was still coughing. It had the same symptoms as a person with postnasal drip.

Harvey decided to stop at a rest area for natural relief and an ice-cold drink from the water-cooler. While he was inside he tried to call his roommate to let him know he was having problems but got no answer. He wasn't to sure if he wanted to stop where he was while it was still daylight or risk a night-time breakdown on a very lonely stretch of dark, inter-state highway. He chose the latter; as there were several things that needed to be done the next morning.

Mr. Norman chose to continue his journey to O'burg, as the natives of the quaint little St. Lawrence River town call it. For the first few minutes his old car was running great. *Maybe it just needed to cool down for a while,* were his thoughts. He was soon to find that fate was going to play a big role in his future. His car however, had a mind of its own this particular night.

# *Chapter Three*

"WHAT ARE YOU DREAMING ABOUT, Harv?" Nancy was watching as her husband was negotiating the big Oldsmobile through the hills and curves of the southern tier of New York State. He seemed to be in a trance; just staring out the window watching the barely visible white lane markers pass by in a blur.

"Wasn't doin' much dreaming. Just thinking about what Kelly had to say about the place in Daytona that's up for foreclosure."

"You wouldn't be interested in that would you? We're pretty much settled in O'burg, in case you hadn't noticed. How in the world would we get everything in that house packed up? The place is huge!"

"I probably would not be. It would have to be exceptional before I would buy it. The other side of the coin is, if it were exceptional, it probably would not be up for foreclosure. So, to answer your question, no, I don't think I...."

His answer was cut short by a large pothole, covered over by a snowdrift. The jolt and the noise were tremendous. Harvey pulled the Oldsmobile over to the side of the road. He knew something very serious was wrong. It was vibrating so badly he thought the car would come apart before he could get it stopped.

Harvey reached behind the seat and got his London Fog overcoat with Rabbit fur lining, and also his stocking cap. The temperature gauge on the left side view mirror was still reading minus ten degrees. As soon as Harvey got out of the car he knew he was in a world of hurt and they would most certainly have to be towed. The snow was blowing and drifting in that particular area of the Interstate. He could barely see 50 feet in front of him. With the wind chill factor at minus 30 degrees, it did not take him long to realize standing outside trying to flag down a passing motorist was totally useless. Icicles were hanging on his nose and ears; he was on the verge of frostbite. He wasted no time getting back into the car.

"Well, Nancy, we are here for a while unless we can get a tow. But the only way we are going to get a tow is if someone goes to look for a telephone. I will go as soon as I warm up." Harv no sooner got the words out of his mouth when his wife got all over him like a cheap suit!

"I am not going to let my husband out alone in this weather!" she said, the anger growing inside her.

"Well, I am sure not gonna take you with me! Honey, it's ten below zero out there! I don't like the idea either, but I think we have no other choice but for me to go. I'll leave you the keys to the ignition. Don't forget to crack the windows when you run the engine. These are perfect conditions for asphyxiation. Don't worry, I'll be fine. One thing about living in O'burg, it teaches you how to dress in the winter."

Harvey was out of the car like a streak before another comment could be uttered from his wife's mouth. He started walking through the whiteout. There was not new snow falling, as Harv could look straight up into the sky and see blue through the blowing and drifting white curtain. As long as he kept his stride up he could keep warm, but he soon became tired. When he slowed down, the chill seemed to start at his bones and work its way outward. He was hoping he could avoid frostbite, as it was a very unpleasant experience, as he well knew from his boyhood days.

Just before shutting their engine down in their Oldsmobile, they were listening to a country-western station from Whitney Point, N.Y. "The coldest day this winter," the D.J. had said.

*Great! That's exactly what I did not need to hear,* he mused to himself. *I wonder how far I will have to walk before finding an exit. I hope I didn't just pass an exit when we had our mishap.* Harvey was trying not to think of all the possibilities of what might happen to him walking in this subzero weather. As he continued his trek in what seemed like Arctic weather, he let his mind wander a bit. It was almost like his mind had picked up where it left off before Nancy asked him what he was dreaming about. Harvey's face formed a smile, almost a pleasant, relaxed expression. Thoughts of his 1964 Olds Cutlass went through his mind. Every Saturday was as Harvey put it in his younger days, "Cutlass Day." This was the day when, rain or shine, he would spend the entire day working on his car. On Friday evening he would set his alarm for 7:30 a.m. Every Saturday started the same way for months. Bacon and eggs with coffee and either orange or grapefruit juice. Then, like clockwork it seemed, at or very close to 8:30 the water hose and bucket of soapy luke warm water and sponge were set and the wash process was begun.

After thoroughly drying the car with a chamois cloth, a fresh coat of wax was applied. This took the young Harvey Norman up to roughly 2:00 p.m. After a lunch break the inside of the "Cutlass" was given the once-over.

Harvey's neighbors went through a very similar ritual at the same time he was going through his. They would stand at the chain link fence that bordered the two properties and pick and tease at Harvey, trying to get him to forget that car and join their outings and activities. Ironically, though, they were the first ones to gawk and point at the "classic" when he drove by.

Harvey had always dreamed of showing the old "classic," and what a true classic she was. It's now thirty years old, sits in a dark corner of his garage, with just a trifle over 40,000 miles on the odometer. For many years after he cancelled his insurance policy on his gem he was faithful in keeping the engine tuned. But, as the days became longer with a growing business, and a wife, his priorities naturally changed. The old car somehow seemed to become just an "Old Car." The tires became flat. The paint began to flake and the finish dulled. Harv hadn't forgotten his old beauty, just wasn't able to find time for it. Nancy kept after him to either sell the 'clunker,' as she put it, or fix it so it will run.

*She just has no appreciation of a gorgeous old car,* were his thoughts.

* * *

That last thought snapped him back to reality and his look of pleasure seemed to vaporize. His thoughts returned to the car and Nancy back on the roadside. Harvey had lost all track of time during his recollection. His feet were still moving across the ground, but the only way he knew that was by looking down to verify they were still attached to his legs. His feet were totally numb, and he now feared frostbite. Icicles were forming under his nose and his lips were chapped to the point of cracking. He had just now realized the discomfort he was experiencing. Thoughts of sitting on the guardrail for a rest crossed his mind but he knew it might mean death from exposure.

Just then, he heard a horn, a loud air horn coming from behind him. Moments later he felt the rumbling of the ground under his very unsteady legs. From behind him, coming out of the white curtain of blowing snow were two headlights of an eighteen wheeler. The passenger door was making its opening swing before the big rig came to a complete stop. The driver yelled something to Harvey. He didn't comprehend what it was, but was hoping it meant 'hop in.'

"Where y'all goin' pal? You sure picked a heck of a morning to go hiking on the freeway! What are you doing out here in this weather? Saw a car back up the road 'a fer piece.' That wouldn't be yours, would it?" The old man wouldn't let Harvey get a word in edgewise.

The driver of the truck was a big, burly, bear of a man, carrying a heavy North Carolina accent. He had at least a three-day growth on his face and a scent as though he had not seen a shower in a week. But, at this point, he was the sweetest sight Harvey Norman had seen in what seemed like an eternity.

"You sp...sp...spoke of a c...c...car up the road." Harv was trembling and shivering so fiercely he could barely speak. "Did you notice anything or anyone around it?" Harv was extremely concerned about his wife in the subzero weather.

"No, nothin peculiar. The windows were getting steamed up so I couldn't tell a whole lot of what was going on inside. Did notice some exhaust, looked like whoever it was is running the engine. Why do you ask, you know em?" The big trucker had a look of curiosity about him. He kept the rig pegged right on forty miles per hour. They were sitting just high enough in the cab to see over the wall of white. As far as they could see there were no exits or exit signs.

"Yeah," Harv began. "I know them. That's my wife in there. We had a little problem with a pothole a little ways back. I think it ruined our right front wheel. That reminds me, how did you know I was out here?" Harvey Norman was warm enough now so he could at least talk straight. He realized, too that he wouldn't have lasted much longer in the cold.

"Well, ah were able to notice a person in the right

front seat. Ah couldn't tell what kind of person, but didn't figure it mattered. Most cars here don't drive from that side. Ah reckoned you was walkin out here somewhere, so I just drove alongside the road till ah found ya."

The more Harvey's ears unthawed the more he heard the truckers' heavy accent.

"What were ya intendin ta do out here anyway?"

"Well, when we broke down I really thought I was the only person dumb enough to be traveling. So, the only way we were going to get any assistance was for me to walk to an exit." Harv wasn't prepared for the trucker's response.

"AN EXIT!!! You were walking to an exit?! Boy, do y'all know how far that is? Y'all was lookin at another fifteen miles. Unless you got insulation ah ain't seein', you never woulda made it. Man, someone sho is lookin out for you!" Harv just sat back and sighed. The old man was starting to sing what sounded like a backwoods folksong. He wasn't too sure about someone looking out for him but he was sure happy to see that old country-boy come along when he did.

# Chapter Four

NANCY WAS PATIENTLY WAITING BACK in the car. She had run the engine for a bit to warm up, but then shut it down. Her husband had always told her that idling an engine for long periods could be hard on it, such as fouling the plugs. *I wonder what he means by the 'plugs'?* she thought to herself.

Many thoughts crossed her mind since Harv had disappeared into the solid white murk. The number of cars that passed them by in the last couple hours you could count on one hand. She wondered if Harv was able to see any of them.

Nancy went digging through her personal belongings that she had with her inside the car. *I think I'll catch up on some letter writing for a while,* she thought, trying to find something hard surfaced to write on. As she began to write to Kelly McGraw, her concentration level soon decreased and her mind wandered. She was remembering the night she and Harvey met. A thin smile crossed her lips as she thought how something more than fate brought those two together. Her Mom and Dad were having a barbecue and picnic for a few people from church, she recalled. They had a large turnout, 75 had shown up if her memory had served her correctly. That particular afternoon in May that year was the warmest they had had yet, pushing 90 degrees. "I must have consumed more iced tea in that afternoon than I did the whole rest of the summer," she remembered. Soon after dark that night after what must have seemed like a drum full of that refreshing drink, her bladder started to protest. Nancy excused herself from her guests and went into the house for relief. When she exited the restroom the doorbell was ringing. Nancy and her mother met about halfway to the door. "I'll get the door Mom. Go ahead back outside," Nancy said to her mother with a wink. Her mother pivoted to the opposite direction and headed for the back door. Nancy walked over to the front door, straightened the throw rug with her foot, turned the knob and opened the door. Her eyes met with probably one of the most handsome men she had ever seen. He was about 6'1" with dark hair and a medium build. When he removed his glasses, deep blue eyes were revealed, carrying such bags under them that his nose looked like it was wearing a saddle.

"Can I help you sir?" Nancy asked the rather tired looking stranger.

"Yes, miss, ah... ah...."

"Caldwell, Nancy Caldwell."

"Miss Caldwell, I wonder if I might use your phone."

"Sure mister...." Nancy paused for a moment hoping

to arouse his name without having to ask for it.

"Oh, I'm terribly sorry," he said looking for the telephone. "My name is Harvey Norman. Please accept my apologies regarding my appearance. It's been a long day of meetings down in Watertown. Then, I had car trouble all the way back. I thought it had corrected itself so I kept going, but it died about two miles back up the road. This was the first house I came to."

Harvey heard sounds of laughing and looked out the back windows at what seemed like an army of people. "I'm sorry if I caught you at a bad time," he said smiling at Nancy.

Nancy put her left arm around his back and took his right forearm in her right hand, leading him to the sofa. "Please sit down, I'll bring the phone to you. You look as though you are ready to collapse."

Nancy walked to the back door and motioned for her mother to come inside. Then she picked up the telephone and took it to the visitor. When she arrived back at the sofa, their guest was sound asleep.

"Whoever he is, he looks plum tuckered out!" Nancy's mother was standing behind her and to one side looking on at the situation. Nancy was in such a state of awe at this handsome arrival that her mother's voice startled her back to reality. "I'm sorry, I did not mean to startle you. I thought you knew I was here."

"Well, I knew you were on your way, but I guess I didn't think you'd be here so soon. Do you think I should wake him or let him sleep?"

"It's up to you, Nancy," her mother said.

Nancy's mother was always a very friendly but

reserved woman, with a very dry sense of humor. But, every once in a great while she would come out with something that totally blew her daughter off her feet. "Nancy, I must say, that with the exception of your father, our uninvited, but totally welcome guest is probably the most gorgeous creature I've seen in a long time. Furthermore, if you don't offer him a ride home, I just may beat you to it!" Nancy's initial reply was a look of total astonishment.

"Mom! I can't believe what I just heard!" There was a long pause. "I think I'll take you up on that offer." Nancy produced a smile at that moment that would have charmed the shoes off a horse!

Nancy walked over to the snoring Mr. Norman. "Sir, I brought you the phone. Could I offer you something to eat or maybe a cold glass of iced tea?"

"Huh? Oh, yea...golly! I fell asleep! That sure wasn't very mannerly now was it?

By initial actions, Nancy could see that this man was very well educated and had done a great deal of traveling.

"Mr. Norman, I would like to offer you a ride home and would be hurt if you didn't accept."

"Well, I certainly would not want to hurt the feelings of a pretty young lady like yourself. I accept your invitation, and I certainly do appreciate it."

* * *

Nancy tried to knit but could only fumble with the needles. She tried to read but couldn't concentrate long enough to comprehend more than just words. Nancy sat and looked at the blizzard going on outside, her mind wandering. Her thoughts drifted back to a time shortly after she and Harvey met. They had been dating for several months, and were getting serious. The conversation of marriage and having a life together had come up several times. Nancy had always had a fabulous relationship with her mother and even though they did not always agree on everything, they were always able to talk about anything to each other. One evening after dinner, Nancy approached her mother and mentioned that they needed to chat about something. Mrs. Caldwell was in the process of cleaning the kitchen and brewing a pot of tea, to be enjoyed by the fireplace during her quiet time.

*Nancy, why don't you fix yourself some tea and join me by the fire. It's so much nicer to talk there.* Nancy could remember the conversation like it had happened only yesterday. Nearly as she could remember, she went to the cupboard and retrieved a cup, and put it next to the stove. As she was walking past the kitchen table to retrieve a pan to boil water in, she saw her Mother's Bible laying on the kitchen table, already open to the appropriate passage. As Nancy read the passage of scripture, she sat in the chair next to the kitchen table. In a few minutes her mother came out from the fireplace and sat next to her. Nancy was just staring into space.

"Nancy, I know you think you love him, but be reasonable. I for one know that he is very materialistic, as well as being a non-Christian. If you marry him, and commit the rest of your life to him, you will be at odds with him from now until one of two things happen. One, you part due to death, or he becomes a Christian. Nancy, if he does not become a Christian, you are going to be in for a long and miserable life. Honey, I don't mean to spoil your dreams, but I just don't want to see you get hurt."

As Nancy looked out at the blizzard, her husband gone into the white murk, quite possibly never to be seen alive again, she was realizing that after all of these years her mother was right. Her mother had known what was best for her and she had doubted her. She was now wishing that she could take all that back. Nancy was realizing that wisdom is not something that you can read out of a book and learn it, but it comes from living life and staying in the Word. She and Harvey had married against her Mother's wishes, and without having 100 percent approval from their pastor. Like she had been warned, her life up until now had been for the most part miserable. The only hope she had was to pray for her husband daily, and she had, several times a day.

Finally she opened her purse and began digging. Several years ago someone had given her a small pocket size New Testament and Psalms Bible. She didn't even know if it was still in there or not. She started hauling stuff out of her purse, almost in a state of panic. She finally found it all the way at the bottom. She took it out and turned to her favorite passage, the 23rd Psalm.

> The Lord is my shepherd; I shall not want.
> He maketh me to lie down in green pastures:
> He leadeth me beside the still waters.
> He restoreth my soul: he leadeth me in the paths

> of righteousness for his name's sake.
> Yea, though I walk through the valley of the shadow of death, I will fear no evil: for thou art with me; thy rod and thy staff they comfort me.
> Thou preparest a table before me in the presence of mine enemies: thou anointest my head with oil; my cup runneth over.
> Surely goodness and mercy shall follow me all the days of my life: and I will dwell in the house of the Lord forever.

Nancy no sooner finished the passage when she heard a siren. It was faint and barely noticeable at first, but got considerably louder with the passing seconds. As she looked out the back window she could see that the visibility had improved and she was able to see an approaching police car. By nature her mind thought of only bad news, how he was probably going to tell her that her husband had been found frozen to death in a snow-bank! Her heart began to pound with fright and her mouth felt like she had been sucking cotton balls.

As the police officer approached the car, Nancy's fear grew with each passing second. He motioned to her to roll her window down. She rolled the window down inch by inch. The wind howled into the warmth of the car, blowing her hair in every direction. In time of fear and panic the human mind tends to slow down. Her every movement seemed to be in slow motion.

"Are you Mrs. Harvey Norman?" He asked in a surprisingly friendly and cheerful manner.

"Y.... Yes, I'm Mrs. Norman." Nancy was frightened beyond the point of speech.

"Well, I kind of figured you were. This is the first car I've seen in ten miles! I have strict orders from your husband to...."

"He's alive?!!!"

"Oh, very much alive and kicking! He wants you to come with me."

Nancy was immediately overcome with joy. She quickly gathered up her personal belongings and proceeded to the police officer's car, which was parked 30 feet behind.

# Chapter Five

AS THE POLICE OFFICER DROVE SOUTH towards Whitney Point, Nancy was asking how he found out about her.

"Well, apparently Mr. Norman got a ride with a passing trucker. He got off at Whitney Point, took him to a gas station and...."

As the officer glanced over at Nancy for eye contact, he saw a once very worried spouse, who was now very relieved, and also sound asleep. He didn't bother to finish what he was saying, but just let her sleep.

* * *

Upon arrival at the gas station, Nancy no more than got the door open when Harvey swept her off her feet and hugged her and kissed her as though not seeing her in ten years. They both had tears streaming down their face.

The mechanics had been waiting for Nancy's arrival in the police car. Harvey had been inside the waiting area of the gas station, a local paramedic, who had stopped for gas, was tending to his frostbitten feet. The service-station attendant had driven to a local diner, ordered hot soup to go, and given it to Harvey for his chilled insides. The attendant suggested to the Normans that they wait at the station while the two mechanics and tow truck driver went to retrieve their ailing car. Very little time elapsed before Harvey and Nancy replied with an acceptance.

* * *

Harvey and his spouse were sitting in the waiting room of the service station pondering their thoughts. Several minutes passed since the tow truck and mechanics left. The attendant went about his duties. Harvey and his wife were essentially alone in the room.

"Honey, what's wrong?" Nancy had glanced at her husband, sitting in the chair trying to look inconspicuous, with tears streaming down his cheeks.

"I can't stop thinking about something, well, actually a lot of things," he said, desperately trying not to let his macho image come crashing to earth. "Do you have any idea how close you came to being a widow today? I was just getting ready to sit on the guardrail to rest when that trucker came by. If I had been on the rail he would not have seen me. If he had not seen me, well..." his voice trailed off, choking back tears.

"Harv, I tried to tell you not to leave the car, but before I could speak you were gone! I was scared to death, thinking I would never see you alive again. The more I think about what happened today the more I wonder why I tried so hard to stop you. You didn't listen to me today, you haven't in the past, and knowing you with that oversized ego of yours, you probably never will listen!" With that, Nancy jumped to her feet, spun around and stared out the window of the service station. Possibly five minutes passed without a word from either of them. Nancy was just staring at the little snow-laden community of Whitney Point. She was deep in thought when her husband's arms reached around her middle from behind. He buried his face into her neck. "You are absolutely right," he said. "Anytime I should have listened, I didn't. My damned ego has always taken over with the 'I can handle anything' attitude. Do you think you can ever see it to forgive me?"

Nancy turned around and gave him a big bear hug, then held him close, their faces nose to nose. They kissed and hugged each other for several minutes when she finally broke the passionate silence. "I already have forgiven you darlin, I already have!"

# Chapter Six

"MR. NORMAN, YOU ARE MORE THAN welcome to take my old Ford down to the diner." The mechanic, who was working on a car out in the first of three bays, had come in for a break. Harvey and Nancy looked at each other waiting for one of them to decide.

"How long do you think it will be before our car arrives?"

"Well, Mr. Norman, judging from what you said was wrong, they'll have to get it jacked up and put the dolly's under it, then it will be a very slow tow back with these road conditions. I would say, that if you and your lovely wife want to get something to eat you should have plenty of time. When it does arrive, we'll be putting it right in the garage so we can get you back on the road as soon as we can." The mechanic was desperately trying to get the grease off from his hands while talking to the Normans.

"Well, if you're sure you don't mind if we borrow your truck we would be interested in some breakfast.

We ate early this morning but I seemed to have burned it off with my little excursion this morning." Mr. Norman cracked a rather sarcastic smile.

"Yeah, some little walk. Somebody's really looking out for you today. The key to the ignition is under the seat. Be careful of the clutch, Mr. Norman, it's a little squirrely at times." With that, the mechanic went back out to the work bay to whatever it was he was doing.

Harvey and Nancy bundled themselves for the cold air and headed for the old Ford truck. When they started down the road they looked like they were riding a bucking bronco. "Boy, that country boy was right when he said this clutch was tricky. I thought I could drive anything."

"Harv, how far is the diner? This snowstorm is terrible!" She was thinking more thoughts than her mouth could speak. "Are you sure we're safe in this truck? What if we mess this one up?"

"Nancy! If you would stop flapping your gums for merely an instant, I could get a word in!" Harv looked at his wife with eyes that seemed to say, "You know it bugs me when you ramble like that!"

"To answer your questions, yes we're safe, no it is not far, yes we'll be there soon, and I'm hungry enough to eat a cow!" The Normans were laughing and carrying on like children when they pulled up in front of Ma's Diner. It stood to reason that on a miserable winter morning like they were experiencing that they would have the place to themselves. Nope. Everyone and their brother seemed to have descended onto this centrally located dining establishment. Parking places were few and far between. After trudging through what to them must have seemed a mile, really being only 150 feet, they were more than just relieved to feel the warm cozy air on their faces when they entered.

"Good morning! Welcome to Ma's place!" The greeting was warm and cheerful. "Sit anywhere you like, and I'll be with you in just a second." Harv led the way, Nancy now wide-awake, followed close behind. They made themselves comfortable in a small corner table in the far end of the dining room. No sooner were they planted in their chairs did the waitress appear with two glasses of ice water. "I realize ice water is probably the last thing on your mind but it might quench your thirst until the coffee is done. We should have bought stock in Maxwell House this week, the way we have been selling it this morning!" The waitress was studying the Normans with intense interest. "Sir, by the looks of your red cheeks and white fingers you could use about a dozen cups of hot coffee! Worst blast of cold air I've seen in a couple years."

A chill went through Mr. Norman's body, as he slowly became accustomed to the 72-degree temperature in the diner. Reflecting on the events of this morning he began to shiver, partly from the temperature change, mostly from nerves. He had not noticed that it was his turn to order. Nancy had already ordered, and was sipping her coffee. "Harvey! It's your turn to order!" She said, almost shouting. Nancy called her husband's name several times. He was in a trance-like stupor. Finally, wearing a look of frustration she tugged on his arm and poked him in the ribs at the same time.

"Oh, I'm sorry," he said. "There I go daydreaming again! I believe I would just like a cup of hot cocoa and an English muffin. Our car is in the shop, or rather it's on its way there, so we'll more than likely be in again before the day is over."

The mood of the Normans, especially Harvey, was making the minutes drag to hours. As busy as the restaurant was it was very understandable that the service was slow. Under normal conditions Harvey would have been jumping up and down beside himself with impatience. Nancy fully expected her husband to march over to the waitress station, ask for the head waitress, and demand better service. She expected him to follow with a speech about his time being too valuable to be wasted sitting in a restaurant waiting for bad service. Her expectations were brought to a halt when her husband just kept staring out the window at the snow.

"He was right!" Harv said it so softly that he barely heard himself.

"Honey, did you say something?" Nancy asked him out of curiosity. She turned toward him; he was neither responding nor speaking. "Harv, I thought you said something, but I guess I'm hearing things today. It's been a long day and it isn't even noon." The family directly behind Harvey had finished their meal and were gathering their belongings. The group of businessmen who were occupying the booth behind Nancy were also in the process of leaving. In five minutes the Normans had the whole south side of the restaurant to themselves.

"Harv, now that the place is nearly deserted, do you think you could open up a little. I know you said something a few minutes ago, something is on your mind. Any other time you'd be jumping up and down demanding better service."

"You are right again, Hon. I was pondering my thoughts and I guess one slipped."

"Do you plan to keep it to yourself or are you going to share it?" Nancy said it with a great deal of sarcasm, but with the warm smile she was wearing, her troubled husband could not help smiling back.

"Two times this morning, two different people have told me that someone or something was looking out for me. As I sit here reflecting on the events that have taken place so far, maybe they were right, maybe it ain't just dumb luck."

Harvey looked at his watch. The action was more a force of habit than a need for the time of day. Nancy was collecting her thoughts. She wanted to talk to her husband about her faith and beliefs. For ten years of marriage that has been her primary goal. For ten years he has wanted absolutely nothing to do with religion or the like.

"You and I got married. You were happy then with this agnostic husband of yours, I do not intend to change now!" That is where the conversation was always left, again and again, year after year.

# Chapter Seven

HARVEY AND NANCY WERE BACK AT the garage an hour and a half after they sat down to breakfast. The news of the car was not pleasant.

"Mr. Norman, your car received an extensive amount of damage. The right wheel and tire were destroyed, the tie rod is broken nearly in two pieces, and we need to replace the A-frame. I'm very sorry to have to mess up your vacation but we will need a week to repair it properly.

Harv was the first to speak. "Do you mind if we have the office with the telephone to make some alternate plans?" He spoke to the mechanic, who was standing by the cash register near the window. Although he was talking to him his mind was in a thousand different directions.

"Harvey, does this mean we'll have to cancel the only vacation we've had in several years?" There was a strong sense of urgency in her voice. From the talk that she had with her husband, and from certain things he had said in the restaurant, she was hoping he was getting close to allowing his wife to share her faith with him.

"Not by any means are we going to cancel this. You know as well as I know that we both need the time away from O'burg. I just have to make some phone calls and arrange some alternate plans," he said walking to the telephone, and picking up the grease-caked receiver.

Harvey travels at least one week out of every month. He is used to booking reservations, travel agencies, and rental cars. Fouled travel plans also play a big part of the business traveler. The first of a long series of calls was to his secretary. Mr. Norman explained fully the situation. He asked her to look up the closest airport served by a major airline. He gave her the number where he was and explained that he had some other calls to make.

His next call was to Hertz Car Rental. The agent was wonderful, one of the few good ones left it seems. Again he went through the whole story. Mr. Norman was ready to rent a car and drive to Florida when the agent on the phone told him it would be much more frugal to rent the car after he arrived.

No sooner had Mr. Norman hung up the receiver did it ring again. The mechanic in the second work bay answered after the first ring. The Normans could see him talking but could not determine what was being said, so assumed the call was not for them.

"Nancy, if we have to fly to Florida you might want to consider some of the items you could leave behind.

We won't be able to take everything with us that we had in the car."

"Give me an idea how much I can carry and I can give you an idea of what I need to leave."

"Most airlines allow three suitcases each person with one carry-on."

The more the two planned their new excursion the more excited they became. Mrs. Norman had never flown, with the exception of a sightseeing tour of the St. Lawrence River when she was very young. Mr. Norman, with his budding interest in aviation flourishing, was becoming more relaxed as the minutes passed. The feeling wasn't something any person could notice, but Nancy could sense it, partly by his mood, partly by the look in his eyes.

The telephone rang again. Mr. Norman stopped dead in his tracks, his gaze fixated on the mechanic with the portable phone. Again, he answered it prior to the third ring. Perhaps thirty seconds passed until he began walking toward the office.

"Mr. Norman, telephone for you, lady named Janice."

"Thank you, sir!"

Janice is a blonde-hair, blue-eyed lady of thirty-five years. Her tall, slender shape, coupled with outgoing personality and charm, are a major asset to Harvey Norman's company.

"Hello, Janice. What did you come up with?"

Janice's voice was strong and clear, a rarity of any call coming from O'burg.

"Mr. Norman, I have two things I think will interest you."

"Well, Janice, you know right now there is only one thing that could interest us, that being a way to get us out of this hole-in-the wall and on our way to Daytona!"

"Mr. Norman, you sound as if you've had a Monday all week! I think you'll like what I have. Is it still bad weather there?"

Harvey and his wife had been so busy trying to make alternate plans they had not looked out the window in hours. When he looked out, telephone in hand, a smile broke from ear to ear. "You know Janice, maybe our luck is improving. The snow is still falling, but it looks much brighter! Nancy, come to the window and take a look out, I think the sun is coming out!"

Mr. Norman forgot about being on the phone. He and his wife got so excited about the clearing weather conditions he dropped the phone on the steel desk in the office. Had he not created the clatter with the telephone he probably would have totally forgotten about Janice.

"Janice, are you still on the line?"

"I'm here, but after that racket I may hang up!"

"Sorry about that, we got a little excited. It's been such a long morning we're all getting a little punchy. So, what have you got for us?"

Harvey could not see the stack of little notes Janice had scattered around from several minutes of telephone calls.

"Mr. Norman, by my watch it's thirty minutes past noon. If you can be at Broome Co. Airport at two o'clock this afternoon, you can catch a USAir flight to Pittsburgh International Airport. Then you will have about two hours on the ground for your connection. At five o'clock this afternoon you will get on another flight that will take you nonstop to Orlando, Florida, arriving at seven o'clock this evening. Janice was talking almost faster than Harvey could write. He had found a legal pad on the desk in front of him. His excitement was building with each passing second. He managed a glance at his wife. She was smiling from ear to ear. He shifted his concentration back to Janice. "When you get into Orlando you need to pick up your bags and go directly to the Hertz Rental Car counter. They have your reservation all taken care of. Your seat assignments are also taken care of. I managed to get you first class service all the way through, which I know you always enjoy. I also made a motel reservation for both of you. It's a small family run place. Not a big one that you are accustomed to but nice just the same. I stayed there when I was there. It's called the Nomad Motel, located on South Atlantic Avenue. The gentleman at the Hertz counter knows you are coming and has directions for you. Do you have any questions?"

Harvey was amazed at how much Janice had accomplished in such a short time. He was trying to think of a way to repay her. His wife came up with the perfect solution that he promptly relayed to her. "Janice, I do have one question. What have you got planned for the rest of the week?"

Janice thought for a second or two, then replied. "I don't think I have too much planned. After the office closes there really isn't a whole lot going on, as you well know. Anything I usually do I get accomplished at lunch hour. Why do you ask Mr. Norman." Janice suspected nothing.

"Janice, what I want you to do now is close up the office for the rest of this week, go home, and don't think about work until we get back from vacation! Also, when you are writing payroll checks this week, make yours for twice what it normally is. I've never said thanks for all that you do. It is the very least that I can do!" Does that sound all right to you?"

The scream at the other end of the line surprised Mr. Norman, as she is normally very mild mannered. To say she was excited would be seriously understated. The look on Nancy's face was of sheer pleasure. Her husband had not had a gleeful look across his face in several months. He looked down at his notes. "I sure hope I can read this when I need to. I did not realize what a mess I was creating." He gathered up his notes and tried to organize them as best as he could under the circumstances. Nancy headed out to the workbay. She started digging into the trunk of their car, knowing she was going to have to reorganize her belongings for the plane trip. The mechanic came over to the car to offer assistance. "Is there anything I can do to help, Mrs. Norman?"

"As a matter of fact, there is! We will need a ride to Broome Co. Airport just as soon as you can find the time. We have a two o'clock flight to get on." The excitement that was building up inside of her was touching her vocal chords. Her voice was cracking with nerves. Her heart palpitated with extreme anxiety. When Nancy had plenty of time to pack and get her things ready she did far better than Harvey could even think of doing. But when she got the least little bit rushed, she basically fell apart. For this reason Harvey knew she could never make a living in the travel industry.

"I would be happy to comply. I'll have my engine mechanic drive you up in my pickup. He talks a bit funny, but he's a good man, just a bit backwoods!" He called his engine mechanic in from the other work bay. He told them about his upcoming errand and about driving their customers as if they were his own children. Then he told him to go over and meet the Normans.

"Howdy, Ma'am! Mah name's James. Friends call me 'Bubba,' I 'spect y'all to do the same! Y'all is needin' a ride to the plane port? Have ya thar in two shakes of a lambs tail!"

Nancy started laughing. She thought, "Boy, that mechanic wasn't kidding when he said his man was a little backwoods."

"Well, thank you, Bubba. We certainly would appreciate the ride. I should be ready in just a few minutes." She headed back to the office where Harvey was just finishing his conversation with his secretary.

"Janice, I can't thank you enough for all the help. I have already given you the go-ahead to take off until we get back. Wait a second, I almost forgot. You said there were two things of interest to me. What was next after our travel plans?"

"Well, Mr. Norman, I don't think it will interest you, but there was a gentleman in this afternoon from Manhattan, a Mr. J. Weiss. Said he was interested in buying your business."

"Janice, if you have his number tell him I'll get back to him."

"All right, Mr. Norman, I will be sure to do that. Have a great vacation and thank you so much for the time off. I certainly do appreciate it. Before you hang up, though, Mr. Weiss did mention a seven digit figure."

"Thank you, Janice, I'll hold that thought." Mr. Norman motioned them to the truck and they headed for Broome Co. Airport.

# Chapter Eight

THE OLD FORD PICKUP WITH ITS RUSTY box and tricky clutch bucked and kicked over the country roads. The country-boy mechanic was busy with the wheel. Older Ford pick-up trucks, especially the 150 series had a common characteristic, a playful steering wheel. This one had about a sixty degree 'dead-spot' as their newly acquired back-country friend called it. With the road conditions what they were, eight-foot snow drifts, blowing snow, and ice patches the driver was not much of a conversationalist. Nancy was in the middle seat, trying to stay out of the driver's way. The shock absorbers were old and the road conditions poor. It was at best a rough ride. Conversation was non-existent. Harvey, sitting on the outside, by the shakey old door, was virtually left alone to reflect on his thoughts.

* * *

Harvey Norman's parents were good people. As a

boy he never had to worry about life's basic essentials. There was always food on the table. He was very well dressed; shoes on his feet, clothes on his back, hair nicely groomed. Never was there a need to worry about money in the Norman family. Harvey came from a long line of successful businessmen. Summer vacation from the private school, at which Harvey attended, was usually spent aboard the family's private yacht on the St. Lawrence River. There was much traveling during the summer months. In addition to his high-class education at the academy, Harvey's parents felt he should be experienced in travel. The upper-class education and lifestyle Harvey was exposed to was all well and dandy. Harvey's father had one major fault, he was an atheist.

* * *

"Atheist." A long pause. "Atheist." Mr. Norman was vocalizing his thought process. This was a technique he learned at the University, which helped him remember details. He had, however, forgotten that he was not alone in the vehicle. His wife was asleep but the driver was very much alert.

"Pardon me, Mr. Norman, but if you need to look up the meanin' of that word, ah have an old dictionary in the glove box." It's left over from mah high schoolin' days. Guess it's high time ah cleaned out that thang! Been near-on ten year since they sprang me!"

With diction such as this, Harv wondered what high school, if there really was one, he attended. Without acknowledging, he reached for the glove compartment and removed the mildew soaked, dirt covered Webster's.

Only seconds elapsed before he found what he was searching for.

ATHEIST: To not believe there is an existing God. Disbelief in something.

"Yes, that definitely sums up my parents," he thought to himself. He then turned back a few pages to AGNOSTIC. After reading and considering the definitions, Harvey Norman concluded that he must be an 'AGNOSTIC.' He had always believed there was some sort of supreme being, but never carried it much farther than that. He knew Nancy was considerably more 'religious.' She often read the Bible, and prayed to Jesus. The only thing he knew about this 'Jesus' person was that he died about 2000 years ago. At least that is what he was told as a boy. "If that is the case," he thought, "what is the use in attempting conversation with someone, or thing, or whatever this 'Jesus' was or is, if his existence was terminated nearly 2000 years ago! That is a good thought to end on, I'm getting confused." With that thought, he rolled up his coat, placed it between his head and the door, and promptly fell asleep.

* * *

Nancy began to stir in her seat. Her nap, though very short, was enough to revive her. As she opened her eyes, her gaze fixed on the improving weather conditions. Her eyes were just getting acclimated to the light when she saw the sign: Broom Co. Airport.... 12 miles. She turned to her right, where loud, snorting noises that sounded like a cow giving birth were originating. In his hands, folded face down on his chest was the

Webster dictionary. Very gently removing it from its resting-place, careful not to disturb her husband from this much-needed rest, she wanted to see what he was looking for. The book was opened to the A's. The left-facing page contained the word AGNOSTIC. The right page held ATHEIST.

*Could it be that the Lord is working on him?* she thought. *Could it be he wants to know the difference between these words? Or maybe I'm just looking at the wrong words.* She knew they must be getting close to the airport, but she would make time. She bowed her head and closed her eyes. "Dear Lord Jesus," she began.

"Dear Jesus, I can feel your presence in this vehicle on this back road today. If you are convicting Harvey I pray he will have listening ears, an open heart, and an inquisitive mind. In your name I pray, Amen." Her prayer was so soft and low only Nancy and the Lord could hear it. The mechanic interrupted the silence.

"Mr. and Mrs. Norman, we are arriving at Broome County Airport. It's currently 1:15 in the afternoon, so you folks should have no trouble makin' yer flights. You have our phone number at the garage. If you would, please call us when y'all get to wherever it is yer goin.' Then we can let you know about yer car."

# Chapter Nine

MRS. NORMAN SITUATED HERSELF IN the waiting area while Harv checked at the curbside counter. A few people were ahead of him in line, which gave him time to get their luggage checked in with the porter. The luggage porter greeted Mr. Norman with out-stretched hand and a wide, toothy grin. The name Leroy was on his shirt.

"Suh, ah will hep you wif yer bags on dis fine day!"

Mr. Norman looked at him rather curiously, then looked outside at the weather, then back at Leroy. "Well, Mr. Leroy, I have no idea where you have been hiding, but my day has not been all that fine! My car broke down on Route 81, I nearly froze to death in that white out, my travel plans were changed, we had to squeeze into a beat-up old pick-up truck and bounce around the country roads trying to get up here on this sawed-off mountain that you call an airport! Then to top it off I meet a baggage-buster with the nerve to tell me what a fine day it is. Hah!!" Everyone at the curb was trying not to look at the scene Mr. Norman was creating. The days events had taken their toll on his temper. Nancy hung her head, hoping that nobody associated her with him. Leroy the bag-porter happened to be the next person, or victim, to come in contact with him. As angry and short as he was with Leroy, the bag-porter never let go of the wide, grin. He kept tagging Mr. Norman's luggage with the proper city codes. He tore off the bottom half of each one, put them together and stapled them to his ticket jacket. Just before handing them back, Leroy scribbled something at the bottom.

"Mistah Norman, Suh, this be yo claim checks. Y'all gonna need 'em at da udda end! Have a fine trip! From the sounds of yo day so fah, it be soundin' like somebody big is watchin out fo you!"

Harvey Norman had heard all of the back woods, diction he could stand. Without even an acknowledgement he left.

As he sat down next to his wife, she only stared into space. He felt bad, deep inside, but his ego would not allow him to admit when he was wrong. He glanced down at the ticket jacket and noticed what was scrawled: Ps.118: 24. *Oh great,* he thought. *Just what the world needs is another religious fanatic!* No sooner had the thought cleared his mind, that they began boarding the flight.

* * *

"Good afternoon ladies and gentleman, welcome to USAir flight1478, non-stop jet service to the Pittsburgh

International Airport...." The public address system was loud and overbearing. Too loud for the small terminal area. "If you need extra time boarding, please step up to the podium at this time." The Normans elected to take the extra time considering Nancy had not flown. Harvey stopped just short of the door. Three identical jets were staring at him all with the same markings. Mr. Norman turned back to the ticket agent.

"Miss, either my eyes have gone bad and I am seeing triple, which I doubt, or you forgot to inform us which airplane is going to Pittsburgh!" Harvey's face reddened again, sweat forming on his brow. "Wouldn't that have been just dandy, after the day I have had to end up in the wrong city!"

The ticket agent took a long, deep cleansing breath, then broadened her smile and looked directly into Harvey Norman's eyes. "Mr. Norman," she said in a soft and low voice, "I am such a fool and sometimes so forgetful. If you hadn't been so kind as to point that out to me, there might have been several people that ended up in the wrong city! Thank you so much for bringing that to my attention. Have a wonderful day and a great flight Mr. Norman!" There was no response Mr. Norman could make. He had been beaten by kindness.

"Yes ma'am," he said, stammering and trying to find the right words. He started to speak again, but just looked at the agent and smiled. Harvey Norman, his arrogance beaten, turned and went to the airplane. As the Normans boarded the aircraft, they found their seats to be in the front row. Nice seats for Harvey, for he had an un-obstructed view of the cockpit as they finished boarding the passengers. He looked up front, toward the galley; the cockpit door was open. He could see the two pilots conversing among themselves. He wondered what they were chatting about. He figured probably they were discussing their route of flight, or the weather enroute, or something else of that nature. The flight attendant came over to the Normans and took drink orders. She noticed Harvey's curiosity at the front end.

"Mr. Norman, would you like to go up and visit our front end crew?" She had one of the prettiest faces and smiles Harvey had ever seen.

"If you don't think they would mind, I would love to. I have flown many times before but never had the chance to look in the cockpit."

The flight attendant cleared a spot for him to proceed to the front, as they were still boarding passengers. It is extremely difficult to go the wrong way in an aisle of an airplane when there are passengers trying to go the other way. When Harvey got to the front office, as airline crews know it, he was greeted very warmly. The Captain introduced himself as Jon. He introduced his First Officer as Mark.

"It's a pleasure meeting both of you. As many times as I have flown I have never had the pleasure of the cockpit tour. Have you got time to answer questions, or am I here at a bad time?"

"Not at all bad! In fact you take my seat, Mr. Norman. Mark will be happy to answer any questions you may have. Make yourself at home, I'm going to get a cup of coffee."

Harvey had a look of awe on his face. So many switches, lights, bells, whistles. The First Officer gave the grand tour. He told Harvey about the overhead switches, the electrical system, the various lights and warning bells. He was able to answer several questions relating to air traffic delays, which Harvey always thought were stock answers for a delayed departure or late arrival. Several minutes passed before Harvey needed to return to his seat for departure. When he did get back to his seat he was wearing an ear to ear grin, much like a little child on Christmas morning. He no more got himself firmly planted in the seat when the forward entry door closed. The airflow stopped and he could hear one of the two jet engines starting. Harvey was taking in everything that was going on around him. He listened intently, as he always does, as the flight attendant gave her announcement on the various safety-related items on board the Boeing 737 aircraft.

Within minutes the Boeing was airborne and climbing rapidly for their predetermined cruise altitude, as First Officer Mark had discussed with Harvey. The cruise portion was somewhat dull, especially since he was sitting in an aisle seat, away from the window. It gave him time to reflect and think. He turned to his wife. "Hon, what significance is a dove shaped tie-tac. I noticed the First Officer had one on." He thought it might be a religious symbol but thought it was worth the asking.

His wife had a very surprised look on her face. She saw the little piece of jewelry as they were boarding but did not mention it. She hoped Harvey would see it during his visit to the cockpit, but figured if he did see it he would shrug it off as cheap jewelry. She prayed he would see it in a different light. Her prayers were being answered. "Harvey, that symbol is very, very significant. It is explained in the New Testament, Book of Matthew, Chapter 3, and verse 16. I have my little one that I carry if you would like to look it up." She looked him straight in the eyes and smiled. In her heart she silently prayed. "Lord Jesus, I can feel your presence again in this airplane. Please give him listening ears, in your name, Amen."

Harvey had never experienced what was going through his mind, but could not come close to describing what he felt like. "Well, Hon, I assume you already know what it means so why don't you just be real sweet and tell me." He had let some of his arrogance slip back in. Nancy was ready with her response almost immediately.

"I would love to tell you what it means, honey! That verse, paraphrased, says that the Holy Spirit showed himself in the form of a dove immediately following the Baptism of Jesus. I assume he wears that tie pin to let people know he is a Christian." Her husband did not respond. There were no words or response he could make to accurately describe his current state of mind. He was feeling frustrated. Several times today 'Bible Pounders' knocked him off his pedestal. This time his ego had succumbed yet again to one of "them," a born-again Christian! He knew his wife was knowledgeable about the bible, but was not sure how much farther it went. He stared at his wife, right square in the eyes, for several seconds. He had no expression and made no sound. Then, he turned and fixed his gaze out the window. Several minutes had passed since they took off in the jetliner. Nancy was deep in thought, looking straight ahead. Harvey's mind was a blur, many thoughts running in different directions. He tried to stay focused in on one thing but failed miserably. He began contemplating the days' events. The fitful nights' sleep, the frigid air when retrieving the morning paper, the near disaster on the slippery road. Then his stroll through the winter wonderland...Harvey Norman had not noticed the subtle effects that comfortable seats, warm air, and humming jet engines can have on a tired body. His head was back and his mouth was wide open, as the sounds of deep sleep were emitted from his mouth. Nancy had a satisfied smile on her face. There may well be hope for her husband yet.

* * *

The First Officer on the public address system brought Harvey back among the living. The announcement was hard to hear, as the pilot was speaking too softly. Something was said about a landing in Pittsburgh in the very near future. Harvey's mind went into gear. He wished they had decided to fly right from the beginning. Financially they would have been a lot farther ahead. Even after his nap, he still could not keep his mind on one subject. He was at a loss for words. He turned toward his wife, much more relaxed after his short but refreshing nap.

"I believe next time we decide to travel on vacation we will just fly from the start. It sure is a lot easier." His tone of voice was considerably more soothing.

"Honey, if we had flown originally, you would not have had your stroll through the snow or that ride in the truck!"

Harvey smiled. "The ride in the truck was kind of fun. But, my little stroll, as you so aptly put it, very nearly did me in!"

Within minutes they had landed and were taxiing to the terminal.

# Chapter Ten

HARVEY, AS HE WAS BOARDING THE connecting flight, looked to his left while going through the forward entry door. He noticed a much larger cockpit than on the previous flight. The flight attendant was quick to pick up on his interest in the front. "Sir, would you like to go up for a visit? These guys are a lot of fun and I think you would be more than welcome." Harvey smiled. Actually, Harvey beamed like a little kid at Christmas. He did not really answer, but just smiled and proceeded into the flight deck area. He raised his right hand in a greeting type of gesture.

"Howdy! My name is Harvey Norman. I'm travelling with my wife, Nancy. I travel a great deal but today is the first day I've had the pleasure of the flight deck tours. I looked at the Boeing 737 when we boarded in Binghamton. What is this one?"

"This is the Boeing 727-200 series. But, before we get real technical let's get some introductions out of the way. I'm Captain McAfferty. My friends call me Mac. Please, you do the same." Mac thrust his right hand to Harvey. Harvey took it in his own right hand and gave it a firm shake.

"Mac, it is my pleasure to meet you."

"Harvey, sitting at my right today and assisting me with flying duties is my First Officer. His friends call him Dan, and I think he would want you to do the same."

Dan turned around, and reached the long stretch with his right hand. Harvey had to step forward a little, around the Flight Engineer's seat, to reach. "Dan, it is my pleasure to meet you. Are you flying this time or is the Captain?" Before Dan could answer, Mac spoke.

"Harvey Norman, you seem like a bright fellow but you got somewhat of a short memory! What I said earlier was that my friends call me Mac. I like to be called Mac, not Captain. I'm not much into titles. I leave that to the F.A.A." The cockpit crew, and Harvey included were laughing.

"O.K. Mac, I will try to remember that next time!" Harvey turned and looked at the Flight Engineer. He thrust his right hand out. "Howdy Harvey! My name is Tomas K. Buchanan. Please, call me Tom." Harvey happened to glance down as Tom was making his introduction.

"Hey, that's an interesting tie tac. I don't believe I have ever seen anything like that before."

"Oh, you mean my double question marks! Come up after the flight and I'll tell you the significance." Tom was smiling, really smiling. Harvey guessed he might be of Scottish descent. He had made it a practice of trying to figure out what nationality certain people were by the surnames and by the way they looked. He also had a very comfortable feeling around Tom. He could not place it, exactly, but he knew he would like him if he got to know him.

"Mac, why does this plane have three pilots and the 737 have only two?" Harvey's curiosity was killing him.

"Harvey, you're learning! You called me Mac!" Harvey chuckled. "This aircraft is older and the systems are a little more complicated and less automated. We have a position dedicated to systems monitoring. Don't misunderstand me. Tom is as qualified to fly this old beauty as I am, but his seniority will not allow him to hold the position." Harvey was fascinated. "You look like you are pretty interested in this stuff. You should take it up, if nothing more than just for a hobby. It's a real blast." They were interrupted by a P.A. from the back, followed by a tap on Harvey's shoulder.

"Mr. Norman, you will have to take your seat. We are getting ready to shut the door and get on our way, unless of course you want to stay here in the snow country."

"No way!! I have seen enough snow for one day!" Harvey started out the cockpit door, but turned just before entering the galley area. "Hey, guys! Thanks for the tour. Mac, I may take you up on your advice." With that, Harvey turned and headed for his seat, in first class with his wife.

* * *

The connecting flight in Pittsburgh was an on-time departure, at 5:03 p.m. The Normans had an entire row to themselves, in the first-class section of the Boeing 727-200. Harvey Norman was quite restless and fidgety again. Finally, after they leveled off in cruise and the FASTEN SEAT BELT sign was turned off, Harvey rose from his seat and went for a walk. He could not go very far, but maybe it would take his mind off the days events. What he had forgotten about USAir service is that it starts almost immediately, so walking at all, at least for a while, was totally out of the question. He was forced to stay in his seat. He had a TIME magazine in his lap, which he usually read, cover to cover, word for word. Not today. Page for page, word for word, picture for picture, Harvey Norman could not tell you what was in that magazine. He turned the last page, stared at the back cover, then closed the magazine and gave it a half-hearted toss onto the floor in front of him, simultaneously uttering a long sigh. Nancy was feeling his frustration as well as hers. She stole a quick glance, mainly to see what he was looking at. He was not looking at anything, but more staring through the bulkhead wall. His arms were "resting" on their arm-rests, but he looked stiff as a board. Nancy reached over with her left arm and interlocked his right arm, then interlocked her hand in his. She put her right hand on his forearm, then laid her head on his shoulder. This was one of those times when Nancy did not quite know what to say. This would require testing the waters first.

"Hon?" She said, almost in a whisper.

"Huh?"

"Can I help you with whatever is goin' on upstairs?" As Nancy asked the question, she touched the side of his head with her right index finger.

"I don't know what you can help me with. My head feels like a collection of blown fuses. I know I've had a large ego lately and have probably not been the easiest person in the world to live with. What I would like to know is why am I running into all of these Bible pounders today?"

"Are you asking a rhetorical question or are you seriously looking for an answer from me?"

Nancy silently prayed for God to intervene. "Lord, I need your wisdom and guidance in this airplane right now. I can feel your presence here. I have been praying for many years for Harvey to come to know you as Savior, and I don't want to wreck it now by saying the wrong thing." Nancy was silently praying when interrupted by the crackling of the P.A. system.

"Ladies and gentleman, this is your Captain speaking. We've had some reports of some choppy air ahead so we will be turning on the Fasten Seat Belt sign. If you are seated I ask that you remain seated. If you are up, please return to your seat and make sure that your seat belt is fastened. Our ride to Florida had been reported smooth all day, so we really don't know why these bumps have started. We'll keep you posted. Thanks." The P.A. system clicked off. Nancy closed her eyes briefly. "Thank you, Lord, for helping him stay seated and not try to walk off this stress he is feeling."

"Harv?"

"Hm." It was more of a grunt.

"Do you know what 'Providence' means?"

"Well, sure. Providence is part of the name of an island in the Bahamas chain, off the Florida coast. It's actually called New Providence Island. One of the smaller of the populated islands, but it is the home of the capital city, Nassau. Providence is also the capital and the largest city in the state of Rhode Island. Why do you ask?" Harvey was now looking at the top of her head, resting comfortable on his shoulder.

"Harv, many years ago, one of our pastors spoke frequently of the "Providence of God." Used in that sense I was wondering if you could tap into that cranial storehouse on your shoulders and enlighten me on that phrase. It's something that has never been real clear." Nancy had her eyes closed, still resting on Harvey's shoulder, enjoying the light turbulence, and relaxing to the sound of the wind rushing by the cabin.

"Providence of God? I'm going to have to think on that...." He turned toward his wife, who was now very soundly asleep on his shoulder, arm and hand still interlocked with his. This would be Harvey's time to reflect on the day.

# *Chapter Eleven*

THE CABIN SERVICE HAD ENDED; Harvey was full and somewhat contented, but still restless. He glanced over his shoulder to see if the aisle was clear, which it was. He felt the desperate urge to take a walk and relieve some of the stress, to get his mind off the day's events, to get rid of all of the coffee he had consumed in the last two hours. Harvey walked to the back of the airplane cabin. He peaked through the tiny hole in the aft entry door leading to the air-stairs. He could not see anything and this seemed to frustrate him ever so slightly. There was a young flight attendant there working in the galley. She seemed to sense that he was there.

"Hello, sir! How are you? Is there anything I could do to help." She had a very sweet voice and looked like she might have been from European descent.

"No, not really. I guess I just got curious as to what I could see. When I discovered I could not see anything

I guess I got frustrated. I didn't mean to let it show. It's been quite a long day."

"Well, why don't you let me take care of that frustration! I'll turn the air-stair light on so you can see out there." She reached over to a panel that was sitting on the left side of the airplane. After she flipped the small switch, the light in the aft air-stair well glowed very dimly but lit it enough so that Harvey could see. "There you go, sir, look all you want. I'll answer any questions that you want. If I don't know them I'll ask the guys up front, I'm sure they will know, this old bird is like a love affair with them."

With that she turned, and took a tray of drinks toward the forward part of the cabin.

A love affair with an airplane. Now there is an interesting thought. Harvey had done a little reading about airline life and airline pilots. He knew that once a pilot had flown a particular type of airplane for a number of years that it started to feel like an old shoe to him. He realized that pilots love what they do but had never thought of it as a love affair. He hoped he could spend a few minutes with these "guys up front" when they got on the ground.

When he got done with looking out the air-stair window he pondered flipping the switch on the little panel but thought better of it. He figured he would never out live the embarrassment if he hit the wrong one and dropped the back of the airplane off. But then, if he dropped the back of the airplane off, he most likely would not have to worry about it. That was enough thinking on that subject. He decided to finish what he came back to do. As he stepped into the small bathroom he could not get over the small space that surrounded him. He wished they could make these bathrooms a little bigger. Harvey washed and took the used paper towel, with the dampness from his hands, and proceeded to wipe the aluminum counter tops. His neatness persisted. His polishing habits were from living in his Oldsmobile days. After he finished cleaning his mess and everyone else's, he maneuvered his way out of the small lavatory and shut the door behind him. There was nothing else to look at in the back so he headed back towards his seat. The flight attendant met him mid-cabin, gave him another sweet, European smile, and wished him well on the rest of his flight. He felt a little more at ease, but still had a lot on his mind. His mind drifted, thinking mostly of something his secretary had said earlier today, which at this point seemed to be an eternity ago. She had mentioned a gentleman coming up from the "Big Apple" and looking at his business. The catcher was when she said he mentioned a seven-digit figure. He knew it was worth a good bit of money but had no idea it was that much. He wondered if he could live the way he was used to and the way he thought his wife was used to living. He knew his wife was enjoying the jewels and the maid service at the house and the security of knowing she wouldn't have to worry about her next meal. He also knew they were living in a very rural town. Ogdensburg is nice but not very large. She does not have a big circle of friends around her all the time. If he sold out, he knew they would be comfortable but was not sure he would be able to keep everything. Then he wondered about boredom. If Harvey did not have something to do he became bored very rapidly. He would go stir crazy within a matter of weeks. He needed something to do should he sell out. Enough thinking, time to wake his wife from her little nap. Very seldom did Harvey feel like he needed advice but this was one of those times. He needed to talk this over with his wife. Part of him hoped she would say it was a wild and crazy idea and the other part of him said let's take a chance on it and do it. He gave her a quick nudge with his elbow. She awoke with a bit of a start. When she looked at him she immediately could see that something was definitely on his mind. "What's up, honey? Something you want to talk about?" She raised her eyebrows and flashed a smile at him all in one movement.

"As a matter-of-fact there is. I was wondering what you would think of me selling the business."

She was now, without a shadow of doubt, completely awake! She looked at him with wide eyes and wide-open mouth. Surprise was an understatement.

"What would you do, you would go nuts within a matter of days. You don't even know what your place is worth do you?"

"Well Nancy, Janice mentioned something today on the phone. She said that there was someone up from the city poking his nose around. Something was mentioned about a seven-digit figure. That's something over one million dollars, Nancy. If Kelly McGraw is right about that business in Daytona Beach, we could start over in a warmer climate. Those winters are really starting to get to me. Besides, while we are down here I would not mind checking out that aviation school she mentioned."

Nancy's eyes lit up and a very smug look came over her face. "So, I was right. You are a little interested in airplanes aren't you?"

"Yeah, I am. I think maybe you know even more than I do how interested I am. I would really like to see what they have to offer. I'm still young enough, I think maybe I could take it somewhere, even if I just used it for business purposes."

She was grinning ear to ear. For the first time in months they were on the same wavelength. He had actually asked her for advice. Nancy was thinking that maybe it really was a good idea after all that they attempted to drive. Maybe he got a few things worked out. With the Lord's help anything is possible. Nancy went back to staring out the window. She was trying to work out all the things that had happened to them since the last time they were in a bed. It was almost unbelievable. She closed her eyes and began to replay it in her mind: The early morning, the lost newspaper in the snow bank, the resulting temper tantrum. Then there was the long, long drive to Syracuse. That created an argument all by itself. She figured she would have been fine if she had not mentioned her friend that was meeting them. But, she also figured it needed mentioning. Again, she was between a rock and a hard place. Nancy felt as though she would have busted wide open if she did not get that off her chest. She had known about it for days, ever since she knew they would be travelling on that particular day. Of course that started the outburst in the restaurant. It all seemed to snowball together. Every time something did not go his way there was an outburst, and it did not seem to matter where he was or whom he was with. She was, however very happy to have Harvey meet Kelly McGraw. She seemed a storehouse of information that Nancy perceived was useful to her husband.

Nancy's mind was starting to wander again. The day had been too long for her to concentrate on any one particular thing for any length of time. She began to look out the window at the ground below. As she began to wonder where they were the public address system came to life.

"Ladies, and Gentleman, from the flight deck this is your first officer speaking." A smile came across Nancy's face. She was thinking about the reassuring voice that he had. "I just wanted to give you an update on our progress. We are currently level and cruising at 35,000 feet, covering the ground at a rate of 590 MPH. Currently, we are over Richmond Virginia, which is the Capital of the Old Dominion State. At the current rate of speed that we are making, we should arrive in Orlando right on schedule. We up front are sure you were ready to leave that miserable weather in the North. The current weather in Orlando is sunny skies with 84 degrees. It is our pleasure serving you today, we thank you for flying with us, and if there is anything we up front can do to make your flight more enjoyable please do not hesitate to pass the word. We would be happy to help you anyway we can."

Harvey Norman was smiling, his wife was looking

at him, enjoying his smile, thinking how long it had been since he smiled, really smiled with joy. Nancy did not need to ask what he was thinking about, but did anyway. Reaching over to his seat, she put her hand on his arm. "What's on your mind, Hon?"

"I was just thinking about that P.A. that he just made. It was crystal clear with a resonance in his voice that you don't normally hear on these airliners. I guess you would not appreciate it seeing as how you have not flown. He has obviously had some radio speaking experience."

Nancy raised her eyebrows in surprise. It was the first time today, since shortly after their departure this morning she had not heard a tone of arrogance in his voice. He actually acted relaxed.

* * *

Her thoughts were interrupted when the Flight Attendant came by taking drink orders. When he turned toward the Normans he had an easy-going, down home way about him. With well-groomed red hair he looked very conservative in the uniform he wore, and he wore it very well, neatly buttoned, tie snug against his collar. The only thing that was out of place was a tiny pin on his left lapel. It was an odd looking pin, one that neither of the Normans had ever seen before. It was a tiny cross with a dove flying over it.

"Good afternoon folks! How we doing today? What a great day for flying, wouldn't you agree?" Harvey guessed he was from somewhere in the Northeast, possibly Eastern New York, or Western Massachusetts. It was not a typical northern twang but more of a timbre that he noticed. "What could I get you folks to drink this afternoon? You can find the menu of drinks that we have available in the back of the magazine that's in front of you. I'll give you folks a minute or two and come back to you."

He moved on to his other passengers that were also in the First Class Cabin. Harvey kept noticing his easy, laid back way he had about him. He knew something was different about him, but was not sure what it was. Nancy had no trouble figuring out what it was. It was almost like she could pick them out of a crowd. Harvey began looking through the drink menu. In his current state of mind, as tired as he was, he could not even make a choice as simple as a drink. But, he had to save face. The Flight Attendant came back to take their order. "Well, sir, did you make a decision?"

"No, sir, I did not. I thought you were such a sharp looking and acting individual I would let you surprise me! By the way, sir, what is your name?"

"I'm sorry, I forgot to put my name tag on at the hotel this morning. We had a pretty early get-up this morning." He thrust his right hand out in what promised to be the handshake of the century, exuding confidence in himself and in his job. "My name is Bob, and you are?" The smile forced a smile out of Harvey. "A very tired Harvey and Nancy Norman, from Ogdensburg, New York. We've had quite a day of it. Sorry if we seem a little dumpy."

"Well, tired Harvey and Nancy Norman, it is my pleasure to meet you. You said you just want me to surprise you so surprise you I will!" With that, he turned and left for the galley of the old triple engine Boeing.

Harvey had tried to sleep a couple of different times. He was in a peculiar state of mind. Sleep eluded him, but Harvey was so tired he could not think straight when he was awake. He began to look around, at the people that were seated next to him across the aisle. He glanced over his left shoulder and noticed the folks in those three seats. They were a family, Mom and Dad and a young little girl, probably four or five years old. Most children he had been around on airplanes were obnoxious at best. But this little tyke was completely different. He couldn't figure it out, but she was actually sitting quietly working on a coloring book. Mr. Norman figured she must have been sick or something. He could not see the couple sitting directly behind him and Nancy, but he could eavesdrop on the conversation. It sounded as though they were business type folks and were trying to sort out some of the numerous problems that go along with business ownership. His mind focus went back to the people next to him, across the aisle. You could feel the tension in the air around the couple that was sitting there. They had obviously had some severe problems somewhere during the day. Harvey concluded that it must be an ongoing occurrence.

About the time of the thought of that couple in distress, a very odd feeling came over him. It was almost like he was looking in a mirror at his own life; at himself and Nancy. He was beginning to realize the kind of husband he had been in recent years. The more he struggled to get ahead, to get the things and toys, to get the big house, to get the fine automobiles, to get just about everything he wanted, he was spending less and less time with the woman he absolutely treasured. Often times conversation at the office would come around to the home. Often times Harvey would praise his wife as though the sun set on her nightly, but things were so different when he got home. He was always bringing his troubles home. Harvey had not realized how much stress he was under until he got a chance to think things through today during his brush with death. He was beginning to wonder if there would ever be a way he could make up the lost years to her.

* * *

Bob, the flight attendant coming with his drink, snapped Harvey back to reality.

"Mr. Norman, here is your drink that you wanted me to surprise you with. If you don't like it I'll be more than happy to take it back for you. I don't get much chance to mess around with concoctions. Most folks don't ask me to surprise them."

"Well, let's see what happens, after all Columbus took a chance!"

As Mr. Norman brought the small, round, spill-proof glass up to his pursed lips, his olfactory caught a whiff of mocha and chocolate mixed, but the liquid in the glass was somewhat clear and fizzing. That ruled out coffee. As he gingerly tilted the glass toward his face, not wanting to get too much of something he did not know anything about, the smell of the liquid began to fill his nostrils. Harvey glanced his eyes towards Bob, as he was looking on smiling. The liquid was almost to his mouth when they were suddenly reminded of their location. Out of nowhere, in dead smooth air the aircraft lurched and everything in the cup ended up in Harvey's lap. The sudden turbulence scared Nancy half out of her wits. The turbulence ended for the moment. Everyone was in the process of getting paper towels and napkins to clean up the sticky mess. About the time they were getting things cleaned up and semi-normal the old Boeing started rocking and rolling at a steadier pace. The seat-belt sign came on and the Captain came on the Public Address system.

"Ladies and Gentlemen, from the front," the Captain said in a reassuring, deep, resonating voice. "It appears we have come into an area of upper level disturbance, usually caused by the jet stream. Now folks, the jet stream is a river of high speed, meandering air that carries weather systems across the country. That generally causes some turbulence at these upper flight levels. We are trying to get a lower altitude at this time, but everyone else is in the same situation so we may have to wait a few minutes. My reason for telling you all this is twofold. One, I don't want you folks to be concerned over the aircraft seeming to rock all over the sky like this. Two, I do want you to stay in your seats at all times for the next few minutes until we get on the other side of the jet stream, as it is usually quite rough all the way through it. Thank you very much for your attention. Would the flight attendants please remain seated until I call you. Thank you." A very calm and well thought out speech. Harvey turned to finish his conversation with Bob, but he was already in his seat, and strapped in.

The aircraft began to rock more violently. Harvey looked out the window at the wings. They were flexing three to four feet as near as he could tell. The inside structure of the aircraft creaked and moaned. Nancy was holding on to her husband with such ferocity that her knuckles were turning white. Harvey, not knowing a lot about large aircraft, wondered how the pilots could manhandle this large of an aircraft while it was going through these massive gyrations. He did not know the autopilot was on and would take care of it without any trouble at all. He glanced back over at his wife. Never in all the years they had been married had he seen such a worried look on her face.

"It's O.K., sweetie. I've been through worse than this. It should not last too much longer. Did you listen to the Captain when he came on. Those guys up there have many years of training just for things like this. I'm sure they know what they are doing. He sounded like he has many years of wisdom under his belt."

It seemed to help her frazzled nerves somewhat, just knowing that he still cared. She calmed enough to let her thoughts wander some.

* * *

Nancy was remembering the days during the summer before her wedding. Looking forward to it was the hardest part, it seemed. Making the plans, which never went the way they were supposed to, was the most tedious. She could remember trying to decide whether she wanted a large wedding or a small wedding. A band or no band. An open bar was out of the question, especially in her very conservative background. Did she want eight bridesmaids or ten? All these details had to be worked out in a relatively short amount of time. Mom was very helpful in this. Mom had an unlimited resource when it came to wisdom. She knew just how much help she needed to give, and when she needed to give it. Also when she needed to let Nancy have her space, which is something all girls need when they face their own wedding. Nancy remembered feeling torn. She wanted to spend her remaining time with her folks as much as she could, but also did not want to feel like she was neglecting Harvey.

There were other concerns to. Nancy's mother was concerned about Harvey's spiritual well being. Mr. Norman was very well liked by Nancy's mother, but her mother also knew what the Bible says about being unequally yoked. Nancy's mother had warned her many times about the problems that would occur if she were to marry a non-believer.

"What kind of problems are you referring to, Mom?" Nancy remembered asking that question as if it were only days ago.

"First, Nancy, let's look at your favorite time of the year, Christmas. The lights and festivities are beautiful. The gifts are a lot of fun but are usually soon forgotten. The problems and arguments start happening when the partner who is a believer begins to celebrate the real meaning of Christmas, which is of course the birth of Jesus. Then, the non-believing partner begins to ask questions. The non-believer will without a doubt question all of the time that is spent away from the family for church activities."

Nancy at this point wished she had listened to her mother. This quite possibly was the most important advice her mother had ever offered. But, like all young women her age, Nancy was lovesick. She had a gorgeous, hunk of a man in her grasp, and she could not let his spiritual well being get in the way.

As Nancy went over her thoughts of mother-daughter conversations gone by, her mind began to wander again. She thought of a verse in the New Testament, 1 Thessalonians, Chapter five, verse 22. Abstain from all appearance of evil. Nancy wondered why of all the verses she knew, why is it this one that comes to mind so very often. Had she, for the past several years been conveying an 'appearance of evil?'

Nancy closed her eyes. She had been staring out the window at the clouds below. Her eyelids were once again getting heavy, and as she realized her on-coming sleep, she reached with her right hand, shut the window shade, and let her head rest once again on her husbands' shoulder. Within minutes she was once again soundly sleeping.

* * *

Harvey was still very much awake. He wanted to read, but chose not to reach for a magazine for fear of waking his wife. Nancy had been looking at her Bible earlier and left it at her side. Very slowly and gently, so as not to wake Nancy, he reached with his left hand for the Bible. Earlier in the day the bag porter with the toothy grin and bad diction had written a verse on his ticket jacket. Ps. 118:24. This is the day which the Lord hath made. Let us rejoice and be glad in it. Harvey thought on this long and hard. It could be no more plain. It was not so much what the verse said, but what it said to him.

Harvey began vocalizing his thoughts, as he often did when he was deep in thought. "I'm a jerk! I have wronged more people in my life than I can count. I guess I need to make amends but I do not know where to start." Harvey was now asleep, his head resting comfortably on the top of his wife's head, which was still resting on his shoulder.

* * *

Harvey and Nancy were both awakened at virtually the same time by the sound of the engines throttling down. The big Boeing pointed down slightly, and the air noise around the cabin changed. Nancy looked to her husband for reassurance, with concern in her eyes.

"Honey, look at your watch, and remember what time it was when we left Pittsburgh. It's been just about two hours since we left the gate. Do you know what that means?" Harvey was wearing an ear-to-ear grin. "It means we are almost to the first real vacation we have ever had!"

"Ladies and gentleman, your Captain speaking. I'm sure the anticipation has been high, especially with the nice weather in Florida and the blizzard conditions in the Northeast. We are currently fifty miles from Orlando International Airport, in the descent for a landing at our destination. It's a beautiful evening in the Orlando area, partly cloudy skies, and 78 degrees. This will be our last conversation with you until you see us standing in the doorway at the gate. It has been our pleasure having you folks on board with us this afternoon, we look forward to being able to serve you again in the future. At this time we ask our cabin crew to prepare the cabin for landing. Thank you, and good evening!"

Nancy was amazed at the sight of what seemed like a sea of lights as they descended into the Orlando area. The old triple-engine Boeing was making strange noises as the pilots slowed it down for the landing. Harvey was somewhat more relaxed now, and was looking forward to chatting with the pilots when they landed. Bob, the head Flight attendant was busy. On this particular flight there were a cabin crew of five, Bob in charge, was working First Class, all the rest were handling the duties of coach class.

"Harv!" Nancy turned back from the window to look at her husband with fear and trepidation. "It looks like the wing is coming apart. Something just slipped down off the front part of it!"

"Oh, I know what that does, honey! The co-pilot explained all that to me when I was up front back in Binghamton. Those are the flaps and they are used for airflow control over the wing at slow speeds. In effect, the pilot can re-design the shape of the wing for whatever phase of flight he is in. The pilot said in the cruise part, up high, they leave the wing "clean" as he put it. But, we can not land at 500 miles per hour, so they change the shape of it and allow us to fly slower than...." Harvey was interrupted by a loud 'clunk' beneath them.

"Honey, what was that?!" Nancy was showing a fear of the unknown, a fear that Harvey did not know she had. His thoughts wandered momentarily. *Maybe if I had spent more time with her all of these years instead of trying to get ahead I would have known about this.* Three bells that were broadcast over the P.A. system brought him back to the present.

"Nancy, that first noise you heard was the landing gear being extended, followed by the signal from the cockpit to the cabin crew that we will be on the ground very soon."

Nancy was leaning against her husband for security, but looking out the window. Soon, the airport lights came into view; they crossed a four-lane highway so low Nancy feared they would catch a car with the wheels. The aircraft nose pitched up ever so slightly, at the same time the engine noise decreased dramatically. Within two or three seconds there was a slight bump when the main landing gear touched down, followed by the touchdown of the nosegear. They had arrived, in Florida, after a very, very long day.

Harvey watched the Flight Attendant station as Bob picked up the P.A. microphone.

"Ladies and gentleman, I would like to take this opportunity on behalf of all of us at USAir, and especially this flight crew, to welcome you to Orlando International Airport, serving Walt Disney World, Epcot Center, Sea World, MGM Studios, Universal Studios, and, oh yea, the city of Orlando! The local time is 7:05

p.m., and it is a beautiful evening, clear skies, full moon, and temperature 74 degrees. A very special welcome to Harvey and Nancy Norman, who I have had the pleasure to get to know on this flight. Everyone please remain seated until we are parked at the terminal. Thank you for you attention and welcome to Florida.

Harvey and Nancy were now looking at each other, very close. "Nancy, welcome to Florida." He gave her a light kiss on the lips and a hug. As the triple-engine Boeing pulled up to the jetway, the Normans were experiencing a warm and passionate embrace.

# Chapter Twelve

HARVEY AND NANCY NORMAN WERE the only two people who were left aboard the Boeing 727. As long of a day as it was, the Lord was at work in the life of Harvey Norman. The Captain had been standing in the cockpit doorway bidding his good-byes and well -wishes to the passengers. The First Officer was working on closeout paperwork, and the Flight Engineer was busily working at his panel, shutting down his various systems. As he called it, "Putting her to bed for the night."

As the Captain, the First Officer, and the five Flight Attendants gathered their luggage and filed off the aircraft and up the jetway, the Flight Engineer called after them.

"Mac, would you be so kind as to sign me into the hotel. I'm going to stay and talk with Mr. and Mrs. Norman. Don't worry, I'll get a cab, I overnight here frequently so I am intimately familiar with the Orlando hotels the airline uses."

"O.K., son, just remember the oh-dark-thirty lobby time in the morning," the Captain said, without turning back as he was headed out the jetway door.

It was now Flight Engineer Tom and the Normans. "Mr. Norman, when you were visiting us in Pittsburgh, I could not help noticing you looking at my tie-tac. Would you like to know a little more about the significance of the two question marks?" Tom had a glow on his face and a gleam in his eye.

Mrs. Norman silently prayed. The interior of the plane was totally quiet. *"Lord, my husband is open to the gospel, to your Word. Help him to be humble. In your son's name, our Savior Jesus, I pray."* Having been married for several years to an unsaved man, and having been in several situations where he's been around Christians, Nancy got real adapt at praying with her eyes open.

"Mr. Norman, can I ask you two questions?" Tom was looking at Harvey with a very serious, but compassionate look about him. Harvey tried to stand, but his legs would not allow him. He tried to smile but could not. His mind thought of a wisecrack, but his lips would not speak. It was as though his body was no longer his, but he still could hear and understand.

"Yeah, I guess so," was all Harvey could utter.

"Mr. Norman, the first question is this. If you were to die today, do you know without a shadow of doubt that you would go to heaven?" Harvey just looked at him. He had been sitting on the armrest with his feet in the aisle, but after hearing that question, he was so dumfounded that he involuntarily swung himself around and sat in the seat. He began to sweat profusely, though the cabin was cool. He turned as white as a ghost. His lips began quivering, his eyebrows began to twitch.

"Mr. Norman, are you all right?" Tom had shared the Gospel with many people all at different stages of readiness but had never seen a reaction like this. Several minutes passed before anyone spoke. Nancy could feel the presence of God, the inner workings of angels all around her, all around her husband.

"Tom," he said, then paused for what seemed an eternity. "Tom you have no idea how close I came this morning to doing just that! We broke down on the interstate in a blinding snowstorm. I had this bright idea to walk to an exit for help; much against my wife's pleading for me not to go. I almost did not come back alive." Harvey stopped, his voice breaking.

"So, Mr. Norman, would you go to heaven?" Tom knew Mr. Norman was trying to distract him but would not give up.

"Tom, I do not think you can really be sure, can you?" The door had been opened!

"Mr. Norman, can you excuse me for a minute? I have to go into my suitcase in the cockpit, but I'll be right back." Tom was standing as he was talking and walking toward the cockpit. Harvey sat looking out the window, but not really seeing anything. He could hear his new acquaintance rustling around in the cockpit. After what seemed like an eternity, Tom came back to the cabin and sat across the aisle from the Normans. He had with him a pad and pen, and a very worn, well-read travel bible.

"Mr. Norman, you said you never thought you could be real sure about getting to heaven. Can I ask you one more question?"

Harvey looked at him with mist in his eyes. "Of course," he said in a soft and low voice.

"Mr. Norman, if you had died today on that snowy highway, and God said to you, 'Harvey, why should I let you into my heaven?' What would you say to him?"

Harvey looked away with a look on his face that his wife had never seen before. His bottom lip began to quiver, his hands were twitching. Harvey was still sweating inside the chilled cabin. He reached out to his wife. Harvey stood and took Nancy in his arms and they embraced like they had not embraced in years. Nancy was crying tears of joy but Harvey was sobbing, big body-wrenching sobs. Tom looked on, silently thanking God for what was taking place on this lonely aircraft tonight.

* * *

Several minutes passed as the Normans re-gained their composure. "Harvey," Nancy tried to form words and vocalize her thoughts through a flood of emotions. Years and years of prayers were being answered tonight as the three of them sat together in the first-class cabin. "Harvey, you have always said you thought there was a Supreme Being but never carried it much farther than that." Tears were streaming down her face; his eyes were red as well. Harvey's pent-up anger had flooded out like a broken dam. He was nervous, and experiencing emotions he had not felt in several years, if ever.

"Honey, crying is all right, in fact I am proud of you for doing so. It is God's way of cleansing the soul and allowing one to think straight again." Tom had gone into the forward lav while Nancy was talking to her husband. He had a box of tissues that he set down between them. "Harvey, look at the chain of events that has happened today. The mishap on the highway, the argument we had about you going out. Then you had your walk in the blizzard and the trucker just happened to see you? It was a white out! How do you think he saw you if he could not see the road directly in front of him? God had His angels working for him telling that driver you were there. You told me yourself you were by the guardrail. If you had not been found, I probably would have died also." Nancy was looking her husband square in the face. "Honey, I love you." Tears were running down both of their faces. "More than anything in the world, more than the huge home in O'burg, more than the maid service at home, more than the jewelry and gifts and everything money can buy, I want my husband happy." Tom just listened and silently prayed.

"Nancy, honey, I think I just figured out what you asked me earlier. The 'Providence of God.' Could it be God working in a sort of behind-the-scenes role?" This was the first time Nancy had ever heard her husband mention God, without her having to bring up the subject first.

"Yes, Hon, that's what it is. Exactly! God working behind the scenes! Do you think you might be ready to listen to what our friend here has to offer?" She was smiling a most joyous smile. Harv broke into a grin from ear-to-ear. He knew his life had to change.

"Yea, Hon, I think I'm more than ready!"

* * *

"Tom, in answer to your question, I do not believe He would let me into His heaven at the present time." Harvey still had a lot of anxiety in his voice.

"Harvey, I have some really incredible news for you!" The Normans could not get over the award-winning grin on Tom's face. "In the book of Romans, which is in the New Testament, God said heaven is a free gift. To be exact it is Romans 6:23. For the wages of sin is death, but the gift of God is eternal life! Harvey, the last time a relative gave you a gift did you try to pay him for it?"

A very surprised look came over Harvey. His eyebrows raised and his jaw dropped. "Of course not! If I tried to pay him he would more than likely be incredibly hurt. Likewise would be true if he tried to pay me for a gift."

"Well, Harvey, God feels the same way. His gift of Heaven can not be earned and it is certainly not deserved. But, I think you will see this more clearly when we look together at what the Bible says about man. Again, we are looking in the book of Romans, but back just a few pages, chapter three verse 23." Tom was saying this as he was handing Harvey the Bible.

"You want me to read it?" Harvey was entering uncharted waters and fright took over.

"Sure, Harvey, you said yourself we are among friends!" There was that smile again, and the gleam in his eyes.

Harvey cleared his throat as if starting a speech. "For all have sinned, and come short of the glory of God." There was a very long pause as he stared down at the page. Then, he read it again, this time with emphasis. "For ALL have sinned, and came short of the glory of God. That's me, Tom!"

"You are an excellent student, Harvey! Not only you but me, and your wife, and everyone you come in contact with. There has been only one person in the history of time that has led a sinless life, that was our Lord and Savior whom God sent. But, there is more! Do you have a clear understanding of what sin is?" Harvey very slowly shook his head.

"Most people think of sin as the big stuff. You know, adultery, fornication, murder and stealing. But what sin really means is anything that does not glorify God. If you and Nancy together only committed three sins a day you and everyone around you would think you were qualified for sainthood. But, at three per day that's still 1,000 per year! That is why we can not even hope to earn it, because no body since Jesus lived has ever been that perfect. That's why God sent his Son, to die for us and all of our sins. Harvey, you've still got the Bible. Go to the first book in the New Testament. Matthew, Chapter 5 verse 48. When you find it read what it says." Harvey was busily trying to find his way through this book. As he was flipping pages, Tom's daily prayer request paper fell in his lap, writing-side up. The words leapt off the page. Lord, help my life to be a witness to someone today!

"Harvey, this meeting tonight is called a Divine appointment. God answers all prayers. What does that verse say?" Harvey had just found it.

Be you perfect, even as your Father which is in Heaven is perfect.

"But, Harvey we just established that none of us are perfect, remember?"

"Yes, Tom, I do remember. In fact, looking back on my life. I do not come anywhere close!"

"Right, Harvey! Which proves this, that man can not save himself. Let me find something else in God's word that should make this more clear." Tom took the Bible back from Harvey and started flipping pages. As he was looking frantically for something only he knew about, Harvey looked up at his wife. I'm sorry. He mouthed the words to her. Nancy winked at him and smiled. Then she turned away momentarily. *"Lord, thank you for intervening tonight on this aircraft. Thank you for giving him listening ears and an open heart."* She still prayed for her husband, even after all the years of rejection from him, never giving up.

"Here is what I have been looking for. God told me to turn to Proverbs and I found it!"

Tom was like a kid with a toy.

"Wait a minute, Tom! I've been sitting right here with you all the time, and I didn't hear anything from anybody. Did you actually hear something?" Harvey's arrogance was gone, changed to a tone of curiosity.

"I understand exactly how you feel, Harvey. When I first became a Christian, I had an awful time understanding how people could know when God was talking to them. Then, after praying about it, listening for his wisdom, and many talks with many pastor friends, I finally got a handle on it. You see, Harvey, like I said earlier, God answers all prayers, but he does so in his own time. He will not do so until He sees fit, then only as He sees fit. It may not always be a verbal and aural answer. Sometimes you have to genuinely look for it. The first thing you need to do when you become a Christian is to quit believing in blind luck and coincidence, realize that everything happens for a purpose. But, I'm getting off on a tangent. Take a look at this verse in the book of Proverbs, chapter fourteen, verse 12." Tom again handed the book to Harvey, already opened. Harvey placed it on the armrest and motioned for his wife to sit next to him. Before she was actually in the seat, he began reading aloud.

"There is a way which seemeth right unto a man, but the end thereof are the ways of death." Harvey just sat there for a long minute. "Tom, why do all these sentences sound like they are talking directly to me?"

"That's a great question, Harvey! I'm really glad you asked. They are speaking to you because that is the way God wants it! If you were not willing to hear this tonight, you would not understand a word on that page. The non-believers call this having an open mind. I call it God's Providence...." Harvey jumped to the edge of his seat and looked directly at Tom, eye-to-eye.

"Did you say God's Providence?"

"Yes, Harvey, I did. It means God working behind the scenes, kind of like the way he kept you out of trouble today during your run of what you would call bad luck. I call it God working behind the scenes, preparing your heart and mind for this evening."

"Tom, keep going! You've got my undivided attention. Nancy and I were talking about the meaning of Providence earlier today."

"Sure, Harvey, I would be happy to show you more. This is what it's all about. Sharing this wonderful news with other people. Let me help you find the next verse that I am thinking about. It is located in the latter part of the New Testament, the part of the Bible that was written after the birth of Jesus. The name of the book is 1 John, chapter four, verse eight. Harvey it will be just a few pages back from the end of the Bible." Harvey began looking, frustration setting in a little. The length of the day plus the events was starting to wear thin on his nerves. He turned to Nancy, and without verbally asking, pleaded with her to help him find this verse.

"Here it is." Harvey turned to his wife. "Honey, my life is going to change! I can feel it. I never thought I would say this but I'm going to need your help."

"Hon, you know I will. But right now, help yourself and read the verse." She was smiling sweetly at her husband, trying desperately to hide the tears welling up in her eyes.

"He that loveth not knoweth not God; for God is love." Harvey stopped, and just looked at the page, then looked up. "Tom, I'm not sure I understand that language. Do you think you could rephrase that for me?"

Without hesitation or thought the answer was ready. "What God means, is that someone that does not have a loving spirit, does not know God as Lord and Savior, because God is love. God is a merciful and loving God, but He is also a just God. This means that justice will be served. He must punish for sinning. Now, please do not get confused. I have thrown a lot of stuff at you. It's time for a quick review. Remember when we said that Heaven is a free gift? Remember when we talked about only a few sins a day, and how we are so imperfect, and how there is no body even close enough to being perfect? Remember, also that because we are so imperfect, we cannot work our way to Heaven. So, what this means is that by being a good person, and by not doing too much wrong, you still will not get into Heaven." Harvey looked at Tom with his mouth hung open and his eyes wide.

"Tom, what you're saying is that no matter how much I help people, no matter how much money I make, or what I do with it once I make it, no matter how good of a person I try to be all of the time, it still is not good enough. I still will not make it into Heaven?"

"Harvey, you are one of the sharpest individuals that I have ever shared the gospel with! Let me go on a little farther. This problem we've been talking about has a solution. God is the solution! He solved our problem through the person of Jesus Christ! Harvey, do you know who Jesus Christ is?"

"All I really know is that he had something to do with God, and that all of our dates and calendars are based on His birth, and that He is the reason for the Christmas Holiday. But, I would be willing to bet there is a lot more I do not know." Harvey's voice got noticeably softer. Nancy put her left hand on her husband's right shoulder.

"Honey, as long as you are willing to learn is all that matters. Remember that I do not know anything about a lot of the things you do. You told me a long time ago to always be willing to learn new things. Here's your chance!"

"Harvey, do you want to look up something in the New Testament, or do you want me to find it? I have another scripture verse in mind."

"If I am going to be a good student, I guess I better try to find it myself. Like my bride said, this is my chance!"

*Bride? He called me his bride! He hasn't called me his bride for years. Thank you, Lord, for working in my husband's life today! Thank you also for Tom and his spirit.*

"O.K., student! You are looking for the Gospel of John, chapter 1, verse 1 and then verse fourteen. You will find it in the New Testament, the fourth book, which is the last of the Gospels." Harvey found it quickly this time, within just a couple of minutes. He read it once to himself. In the beginning was the Word, and the Word was with God, and the Word was God. And the Word was made flesh, and dwelt among us, (and we beheld his glory, the glory as of the only begotten of the Father,) full of grace and truth. There was a very, very long silence. Harvey was deep in thought. It was obvious to Nancy that he was deep in thought, trying to take in these two important scriptures. Tom was about to say something when Nancy caught his eye and ever so slightly shook her head. Then, Harvey looked back toward Tom and re-focused his thinking. His ability to ignore his present surroundings came from years of practice and years of being in business for himself.

"Tom, Jesus was one of us! He was flesh and blood, a walking, talking and breathing human being! If everything that the Bible says is true, then everything Jesus said must also be true, am I correct?"

"Harvey, you are the most CORRECT person that I have run across all day! Right now I think more people should go through what you went through. It would make them appreciate life more, and also make them realize who is REALLY in charge. Harvey, what makes Him so special is that He was born of a virgin, His mother Mary. She had not intimately known His earthly father, which scientifically and medically speaking made His birth impossible."

"But, Tom, it says right in the book that it DID happen. With so many of these books in circulation, how can it be wrong? This is really interesting and you are incredibly knowledgeable! What else do you have?"

Nancy turned and looked out the window. Her eyes were welling up again. She had just realized that her non-believing husband was listening, actually listening to the GOSPEL! It was beginning to look like her years of praying, of fasting, of meetings with her pastor, were going to pay off tonight! *"Lord, I know I run the risk of looking a gift horse in the mouth, but it looks like he is going to accept you as Lord and Savior tonight. Please, Lord help him to be a better husband, and Lord, help me to be a better wife."*

"Well, Harvey, I need to tell you why God sent His Son. Heaven was created for us, for people. It is a place for people to go after death. But, when humans started sinning and it was getting worse and worse, God realized we needed some help. To pack a long, century upon century story into a nutshell, He sent His Son, Jesus to die for us. By sending His Son, and having Him crucified, He in effect cancelled all our sins, both past and present so that we can have eternal life in Heaven. This gift of eternal life is exactly that, a gift! The only way you can receive it is by faith. You have to let Him into your life, receive Him."

"But, Tom, I've never had faith in my life. I have always thought things just kind of happen."

"Tom, you have had faith all of your life! You just never realized what it means." He looked at Harvey, watching his puzzled look form on his face. Nancy knew where Tom was going with his illustration. "Harvey, did you eat in a restaurant today?"

"More times than I care to remember! Probably the same for my bride."

*He did it again! He called me his bride again. Could it be he still loves me, but is too stressed out to show it?*

"Harvey, when you were eating in the restaurant, were you sitting down or standing up?"

Harvey looked at him like he was from another planet. "Bear with me Harvey, I think you will see where I am going in a minute."

"O.K. Tom, I'll play along! I was sitting down, so was Nan."

*Wow! A nickname. He hasn't called me Nan since we were dating! His stress is leaving and his mind is back in place. There is hope!*

"Good! Now the big question. Did you send the chair to be analyzed for integrity or did you just sit in it?" Harvey reacted almost immediately. His face wrinkled and he started to involuntarily nod his head in agreement.

"I just sat down...without really knowing if the chair would hold me or not. I just sat down. I guess what I was doing was trusting the restaurant that they would have strong chairs."

"Very good Harvey, you impress me. If ever you would like a business partner call me, I like to work with intelligent people. Let me give you another example of faith. Did the restaurant require payment before or after you ate?" Harvey began smiling, smiling with an understanding of Tom's point. "We paid after we ate. But, they did not know when we walked in whether or not we had money. So, the restaurant had faith in me, just like I had faith in that chair! Tom, it sounds to me like FAITH and TRUST go hand-in-hand!" Harvey had a look of extreme satisfaction on his face, like a pupil who had just passed a difficult math exam.

"Harvey, do you know who Satan is?"

"Tom, I know what Satan is, but I never thought of it as a who."

"Satan is the Devil. Sort of the enemy of God, and His Son, Jesus. For everything that God does, the Devil or Satan will try his best to undo it. Whenever someone receives Christ as Savior, Satan kicks into overdrive. He puts the hammer down. He puts his foot in the carburetor! Do you catch my drift?" Harvey was smiling, Nancy was laughing. She had never heard it put that way before.

"That's great! How could anyone not understand it when you explain it in a way that any male human would understand?"

"I try to keep this very understandable to everyone. If more people understand it when it is explained to them, then more people will come to know Christ! Satan also believes in God. Look at the book of James, chapter two, verse nineteen. You will find it towards the back of the New Testament, after the book of Hebrews and before 1 Peter." Harvey began looking before Tom had finished speaking.

"I found it!" Nancy began tearing again. *"Lord, I haven't seen a fire in him since we were married. Thank you Lord!"* "Do you want me to read it out loud or to myself?"

"Read it aloud, if you would."

"Thou believest that there is one God; thou doest well: the devils also believe, and tremble. Yet another example from the Bible. It says right in that book that Satan believes in God!" Harvey reached over to his wife and grabbed her hand, their fingers interlocked. Nancy's thoughts drifted again.

*How long has it been since we've held hands!!*

Tom acquired a more serious nature about him, all of a sudden. "Harvey, we need to clarify something right now. That is the difference between temporal faith and true Christian faith. Temporal faith is trusting God for worldly matters and Christian faith is trusting Christ for everyday living, for everything that happens in life. Please understand that God and Christ are frequently used interchangeably. They are one in the same. Remember back to the verse from 1 John? The Word was God. He came as flesh. That would be Jesus."

"Tom, is that like asking God for help in a crisis, but not really meaning it, but it was the only word you could think of?"

"Exactly. Be very careful what you ask God for. Remember, He answers EVERY prayer, but He does so in His way and in His time."

Tom was visibly nervous. More so within the last few seconds than the previous twenty or thirty minutes. Harvey started to pick up on the body language, but Nancy already knew where Tom was heading. She excused herself. "Tom, I need to use the ladies room, all that coffee I had to drink on the way down here finally caught up with me." Her husband turned his body sideways to let her out. As she rose to her feet, and shuffled past her husband her eyes met Tom's and they silently communicated. They were on the same wavelength. Tom winked at her. She went into the tiny restroom, closed the door behind her and slid the lock to the OCCUPIED position. At this point, she did not care what the condition of the floor was, nor how clean the lid of the toilet was. Nor did she care what the condition of the air was. This tiny lavatory, in the front of the old Boeing 727, at the Orlando International Airport, at 7:40 in the evening became an Altar of God! She knelt down, folded her hands, closed her eyes, and began to pray.

"Lord, your presence in this place tonight has been miraculous. Thank you for the wonderful day you have given to Harvey, for the eye opening experiences you have shown him. Thank you for opening his heart to your Word. I praise you Jesus, for Tom...I don't even know his last name, Lord, but I know you do. Bless his family. Bless his life as he lives it for you, Lord. The time has come Lord, for Tom to lead my husband in the prayer of salvation. Make him open to it. Lord, help my husband to change his life, to realize that there is true happiness in being devoted to you. Lord, allow me to help in any way you would see fit. I love you Lord Jesus, and I want to always live my life for you. I ask these things in your Holy and precious name, the name of Jesus, AMEN!" She arose, straightened up her clothing, slid the lock to the VACANT position, opened the door and returned to her seat.

"Harvey," Tom began to ask a question but stopped, looking for the right words. "Harvey you are incredibly bright, and I know you have had quite an interesting day, to say the least. Does all of this stuff we have talked about tonight make sense to you?"

"Tom, it makes complete sense! Tell me what I have to do!"

"Harvey, this is your moment. Would you like to receive the Gift of Eternal Life?"

"Does that mean I have to ...pray? I've never done that before."

"I will lead you, you can follow me if you want, or I can pray for you, or you can pray on your own. It is no different that talking to your best friend, which you should be pretty good at, seeing as how most people have their best friend as their spouse."

"Tom, I understand what you are saying but I do not think I have been a very good best friend to Nan. At least not lately. That will change shortly. I think I will let you pray; then maybe I will pray after you. Would that be all right?"

"Perfect!" Nancy moved out of her seat again and knelt in front of her husband, with her back against the bulkhead.

"Lord Jesus, thank you for leading me to the Norman couple tonight. It has been a wonderful and joyous experience to be able to share your Word with them. Please be with my new friend as he takes on a new life! Harvey is a sinner and knows he is a sinner, he understands the Word, Lord, and he wants to receive you as Savior and Lord of his life! Lord, give him peace as he proceeds into uncharted waters. Listen as he speaks to you, Lord. Help him with upcoming trials and tribulations as a baby Christian." Tom tapped Harvey on the knee, without opening his eyes. "Harvey, would you like to pray now?" Harvey did not even answer.

"God... I mean... Jesus, well, I guess if you know everything, you know what I mean." Nancy reached her arm around him and gave him a loving squeeze, signaling her presence. "Lord, I have not been a good person. I have a quick temper. I have ignored the woman I love dearly and promised to spend the rest of my life with. God, I know I am a sinner and I need to change. Tom has been kind, too kind. He has taken his sleep time to help me realize how bad I have been. God, I want you to come be MY God, so I can live my life right." Nancy could be heard sniffling, and whispering her thanksgiving to Jesus. "Lord! I need you as Savior and Lord of my LIFE!" At that moment, Harvey broke down and began to sob. He threw his arms around his wife and buried his head in the base of her neck. Nancy was consoling him as he repeatedly apologized for being such a lousy husband. Tom began to pray.

"Thank you Jesus, for saving Harvey! He is a good man. Be with Nancy and Harvey as they start a new life together. Help me to be a disciple to them. Help them to get involved in a good, Bible believing and Bible preaching church, where you are the head of it. Help us all to keep Satan out of our lives! Thank you, Lord, for allowing me to have a job where I can meet many new people every day, and where I can be a witness for you, every day!!"

# Chapter Thirteen

THE DIRECTIONS FROM THE RENTAL car agency were explicit and perfect. The drive to Daytona seemed endless. Harvey and Nancy checked into their humble, family owned motel, sitting directly on the shores of the Atlantic Ocean. As they pulled into the driveway of the motel Harvey looked up and noticed the sign. It had a symbol of a fish in one corner and symbol of a dove in another corner. As Harvey was parking the rental car and getting out he looked at the sign again. "Honey, I've seen the dove once before today. But the fish is a new one. Are they fishermen?" Harvey asked smiling.

"Harvey, you are so close to being right that it's scary. They are not fishermen but fishers of men. That symbol is called an ictus, with a long 'u' which means Jesus Christ, Son of God. It, like the other symbols you ran across today, signifies Christianity. Either the people who run this motel or the people who own this place are probably Christians."

Harvey and Nancy walked toward the office to check in. They were holding hands and acted like a couple of college kids going out on their first date. Harvey reached the door first, pulled it open, held it for Nancy to proceed through first. Nancy looked at her husband, put on a sophisticated, elegant lady impression and winked at him at the same time. "Why my dear husband, I do thank you!"

"You are quite welcome, my dear lady. Anything for you!" The two of them were being silly. This is a side of Harvey that Nancy had never seen. It was like the whole world had been lifted off from his shoulders.

* * *

"You must be the Normans!" A very cheerful voice came from behind the counter. "Tom, a pilot with the airline you came in on gave me a call and told me to be looking out for you. He said you guys were really wiped out and needed special treatment. If you folks will kindly turn your car keys over to me I will see to it that your luggage is removed from your vehicle and taken to your room. I have your room all set and I think you'll like what we've done inside. Now let's take care of the paper work and get you settled. From the sounds of things you folks could use a good nights sleep." Harvey willingly turned over his car keys. They were handed to someone in the back room. "Here, John, these keys belong to the Normans. Their car is the one right in front of the door. Put their luggage in room 107. Make sure that everything else is set in there too, please." Harvey looked at his wife puzzled.

"Sir, pardon my curiosity but what is all the fuss about? You keep talking about everything being 'set.' Would you mind letting me in on it?" Harvey was trying to be coherent. But at this point, after the day they had, he was barely able to stand on his own two feet. Nancy was leaning on the check-in counter next to some attraction brochures, with her head resting in her hands. She was just about to fall asleep on her feet.

"Mr. Norman, I understand you are a new member to the family of God! That is the greatest thing that you could have ever done. Come down after you have had some rest, tomorrow or the next day, or anytime while you are here. I have a testimony I would like to share with you. But, for now let's get you two to your room. I have the key right here." He handed a set of room keys across the counter, one to Harvey and the other to Nancy. Harvey looked at the tag, memorized the number as he was accustomed to doing, then flipped the tag over. On the other side he saw the two question marks for the second time that day. He looked up and smiled.

"Sir, this time looking at these question marks I can honestly say they take on a new meaning. This must be your way of spreading the gospel."

* * *

Harvey and Nancy walked into room 107. There was a banner flying over the door to the patio. "WELCOME HARVEY AND NANCY NORMAN." Harvey and Nancy stood there dumfounded. In all the years Harvey had been travelling around the country, he had never had treatment like this, and never would have expected it in a small family owned motel. Harvey stood there almost in tears unable to speak. He turned to his wife with misty eyes.

"Honey, do you think you can forgive me for all the years we've lost? Could we start over, and make a new life for ourselves? Could you see it in your heart to let me learn how to be a good husband and eventually a good father?" He was choking back tears, partly due to being overtired, partly due to his aching heart.

"Honey," she said very sincerely, with tears streaming down her face. "I never gave up hope for you. I just kept praying for you, because I knew one day Satan would lose and God would win. You see, being a Christian does not change the outer shell of the person, just the inner self. Sweetheart, you are now a new person! New on the inside even if not on the outside. We have a new world opening up before us. We now walk together, equally yoked, both Christians, both of us a child of God, with a living Savior living within our heart. Now it becomes our duty as Christians, working together as a team, to share this new life of yours and ours together, with as many people as possible in the shortest time possible." Harvey stood there, staring at his beautiful wife, totally speechless.

"Nancy, I don't quite know what to say. How about I don't say anything until we wake up in the morning, whatever LATE hour that might be. One of those wonderful people that we ran into today, which one I can't remember, told me that daily prayer was important, as was nightly prayer. How about you and I start this new life together on our knees in prayer. It will be a first for me and there is no person I would rather share that first with than you." Now it was Nancy's turn to be in tears. Not a word was spoken as they shuffled their tired feet over to the bed and quickly turned the bed into an altar before the Lord. They knelt down, the only sound in the room was the hum of the air conditioner unit, and if they listened closely, they could hear the sound of the surf just outside the sliding glass door. Harvey leaned on the bed, awkwardly folded his hands in front of him, closed his eyes and began to pray to Jesus for his first time. His wife put her arm around him.

"Lord, this is new to me, so forgive me." Harvey was again choking back tears. "This is hard to talk to someone that you know is there but you can't see him. I guess Lord, what I'm trying to say is... well... I've seen something different about my wife ever since we got together way back when." Harvey paused for a moment and stole a peek at his wife. He whispered to her, "Do you think he's listening to this mess?" Nancy gave a nod of approval. He continued to pray. "Lord, I've been a totally useless husband and probably done some business practices that I know deep down inside that I should not have. I certainly have not spent any time in church. I've always left that up to my wife. I guess I figured that one church person in the family was plenty. I think I figured wrong. I truly believe that you used the events of the last twenty-four hours or so to give me a wake-up call. Lord, I'm awake! I'm ready for service! I'm ready for action. I've had a phone call today about selling out the business in O'burg. If that is what I'm supposed to do then I guess you will tell me, although I don't know how because I don't know how to listen to someone I can't see or feel. Lord, so much of this is still a mystery. I guess I'll leave it there tonight. Well, thanks for listening, thanks for being patient with me. Thanks for giving my wife so much patience over the years. Amen."

Harvey looked up and then over to his wife, her head lying on her folded arms, smile on her face, sound asleep. He very quietly pulled the covers to the bed back, then scooped up his sleeping wife and placed her between the sheets. He was very close behind her on the other side. Both Harvey and Nancy were asleep as soon as they hit the pillow. Years and years of prayer had finally paid off for Nancy. Her husband was finally a child of God, a born-again Christian. Her husband now had a non-returnable reservation for a mansion in heaven.

# *Dawn of a New Life*

THE NORMANS WERE IN A DEEP SLEEP when the first sounds of daylight began to creep into their room. Nancy had arose in the wee hours of the morning, looked out the window at the pool in the yard of the motel and saw a couple sitting under the stars. It appeared the two of them were in a deep conversation both talking, then smiling and eventually warmly embraced in each other's arms. In moments they were passionately kissing. Nancy turned away with tears in her eyes. She looked at her sleeping husband. Nancy had been longing for that kind of a relationship with her husband for years but it never happened. Nancy unlocked the sliding glass door and very quietly slid it open, careful not to wake her very tired and weary husband. She stepped out onto the small concrete patio and let the warm sea breeze fill her lungs. It had been years since she had smelled and heard the ocean and spent the next few minutes letting the memories come back to life. When she finally came back to her senses, she realized she was standing on the patio in only her nightgown, then also realized why she had gotten up in the first place. As she went quietly back into the dark room, she left the patio door open slightly, enough so the sound of the ocean would poor into the room. Soon, she was back in bed with her husband and in a very deep slumber.

* * *

The first ray of sunlight broke into the East-facing room at 5:50 a.m. Harvey had always had a knack for getting up with the first rays of the morning, this morning being no exception. Almost as if an internal alarm clock goes off in his head, he is up with the sun.

"Time is money, and days are short. My day starts when the sun comes up. That's when I am most productive," he would always say. The ocean air greeted his nostrils as soon as he was alert enough to recognize the smell. He inhaled deeply, enjoying the smell of the salty breeze coming into the room. His ears perked up when he heard the seagulls playing silly games on the beach not too far from their room. When he got up he wandered over to the partially open door where he watched two pelicans diving for baitfish just off the beach. He looked to the right, towards the south and saw couples walking on the beach hand-in-hand, feet in the surf, all smiles. When he looked to the left, towards the north he noticed a man with a very long fishing rod standing waist-deep in the surf, casting out a baited hook. All of these people were not much older than he. Not much older than their mid forties. But there was definitely something different he noticed, but could not pinpoint what it was. Harvey reached up and grasped the sliding-glass door with his right hand and began to slide it open. He had one foot out the door when his mate suddenly stopped him.

"You know honey, I always knew you thought a lot of yourself, but I never thought I would see the day when you would walk outside in nothing but your briefs!"

Harvey stopped dead in his tracks, looked down, and then looked back at his wife lying in bed. A warm smile crossed his face and Harvey Norman actually broke out laughing. This was the first time Nancy had heard him really laugh in years. Harvey stepped back inside, enjoying a good belly laugh, his wife also giggling. Harvey stood there in the middle of the room, his left hand on his hip, his right hand on the door. He closed the door with his right hand then closed the curtain. Then, an animated side of Harvey came out that surprised even his wife. He puffed out his chest, sucked in his gut, and strutted over to his wife, still lying in the bed.

"Do you think you can find room in that side of the bed for one more person?" he asked in the best John Wayne imitation he could muster.

"Why, my dear Harvey. Do join me!" Nancy was working hard on her sophisticated English accent. A warm embrace followed shortly after he crawled in bed with his wife. An embrace that was long overdue. They gazed into one another's eyes, just enjoying the companionship. This was the first time this had happened in years. Nancy felt like God was answering all of her prayers at once.

* * *

When the clock struck seven a.m., they both arose and ambled off to the bathroom to freshen up and try to recover from the previous day, a day that both of them would like very much to forget.

Nancy busied herself in the efficiency part of the room, the small kitchen, opening doors and cupboards, checking out her surroundings. As she looked in one of the lower cabinets under the sink she found the coffeepot, carefully brought it up onto the counter and plugged it in. For years Harvey had made his own coffee, but now they were on vacation, Harvey was starting to relax some of his ego, and Nancy thought it was high time she pampered him a little. She could hear the water running in the shower and see steam coming from under the door.

*I've never seen him take this long of a shower before, sure hope he's all right,* she thought. Nancy walked over to the bathroom door and gave a light knock.

"Nancy, you can come in if you want, but it's pretty steamy in here!" Harv called from the shower.

"No, Hon, just checking to see if you are all right. I haven't seen you take a long shower in years."

"I haven't been on vacation in years! It is sure nice to be able to stand here and enjoy this water without having to be somewhere."

Nancy walked over to the clock radio on the nightstand, turned it to the first FM station that happened to be tuned in, then walked away towards the kitchenette. She found a bag of coffee in the cupboard with a folded note attached with a paper clip. Carefully unfolding the note she read to herself.

*Dear Mr. And Mrs. Norman,*

*Hope everything here meets your expectations. Our job as proprietors is to please our guests. We live on the property, just behind the office. If there is anything that we can do, regardless of the time of day or night, please do not hesitate to call. It is our pleasure having you stay with us!*

*Sincerely,*
*Adam*

"What a nice gesture. I wonder if all hotels do this or if this is specialized? Harv would know, I'll be sure to ask him when he comes out of the shower. If he comes out of the shower!"

As Nancy was scooping out the coffee with the supplied measuring cup, the radio caught her attention. It was a Christian gentleman with many years' experience in the ministry giving a short testimony. She listened intently as he quoted several familiar verses from the Bible, but there was one thing that stood out in her mind. Nancy was totally riveted to the radio when he talked about God working "Behind the Scenes," the Providence of God as he so aptly put it. He talked about how God uses his angels as messengers, how God will put certain people in the path of a lost soul. The pastor also talked about how God will place a certain chain of events in a person's life. As quickly as he started speaking, he finished and the host came back on the air.

"Ladies and Gentlemen, you have been listening to this mornings edition of "The Pastor at the Door!" Every weekday morning, one of the local pastors visits us for a brief testimony and an insight into life's little secrets...." Nancy turned off the radio, coffee scoop still in hand. Again she stared out the window for a few short moments, reflecting on the day previous, not so much the length of the day or even the dangers involved, but more of what the pastor on the radio was just talking about. Nancy was thinking about how God had worked in Harvey's life, how he had been working in his life without him even knowing or caring. It took a near death on a snowy highway. It took a country trucker who just happened to come along at the right instant. It took a smiling baggage handler at the airport, and ultimately it took a very dedicated servant of God named Thomas who chose to make his living helping people in the airline industry. Nancy believed that these were all people and events that were placed by God.

Her husband interrupted her thoughts. "Honey, I can't find the towels! Can you help me!"

*My husband, the former ego and world traveler wants help!?* "Sure, honey. I'll be right there!" She grabbed a towel out of the linen closet then took it in to her dripping wet husband.

"Thanks, Nan. I don't know where my brain is, I never forget my towel when on the road."

"I know where it is, it's finally on vacation!" Nancy said with a laugh. "Hon, what have you got in mind for breakfast, or maybe you're not even hungry yet, have you thought about it?" Nancy was talking through the bathroom door.

"It's a nice morning for a walk. Why don't we take a walk on the beach and we'll see what we bump into. I saw some other people walking on the beach this morning. They looked like they were enjoying it. Who knows, maybe we will too." Harvey cracked the door, stuck his head out through the steam, looked at his wife, and gave her a toothy grin.

"Harvey, I don't care where we go or what we do, as long as I'm with you. I'm enjoying the new you. You seem like you have a thousand pound weight lifted off from your shoulders and you have gotten rid of your stress almost over night."

* * *

Harvey and Nancy walked out of the sliding glass doors together, hand in hand, smiling at each other. This was the first time in their life that they were equally yoked, both Christians, both with a mansion reserved for them in Heaven. Nancy kept thanking God for His goodness, Harvey was just thankful that he lived through the previous day, and for his salvation. He was also feeling remorse for all the years he had lost with his beloved wife, all the years of selfishness, all the years of missed opportunities just because he was trying to get the toys, to make life "just the way it should be," as he had always said. As they walked past the swimming pool on their right, there were other vacationers setting up their chairs for their daily tanning rituals. On their left was a well-manicured lawn, also containing several beach towels and blankets. A gentleman from the motel, possibly a maintenance man or one of the owners, was busy working on the shuffleboard court, located just prior to the beach entrance. The Normans approached the stairs to take them down to the beach. Harvey stepped back and let his wife go down first, never letting go of her hand. Both were clad in new shorts with matching top and no shoes. A smile crossed each of their faces at the same time as their toes hit the soft, cool sand.

"Ah, this sure beats 32 below zero like it was when we left yesterday!" Harvey was smiling from ear to ear like he didn't have a care in the world. "You know honey, I'm glad we're here. I wish we had done this years ago." Harvey was talking to his wife but never once took his eyes off from the ocean, only yards away from them.

"Harv, if wishes were horses beggars would ride!" Nancy looked at her husband with a grin.

"Where did you come up with that?" asked Harvey.

"I don't know, it just seems to make sense, doesn't it?"

"Now that you mention it, yes it does!" He fixed his gaze out toward the ocean again. They began walking south on the beach, with the relatively early morning sun low on their left side.

"Nan, the saying makes sense, but what exactly is your point?" There was no longer any hint of sarcasm in his voice, just a need to know what she meant.

"Honey, all I'm saying is that you can wish all you want for things in our past to be different but you can't change them. You are however a new person in the eyes of the Lord. Therefore, you and Him working together can change the future. I see an incredible change already, but don't get complacent. Remember that the Lord has someone working against him all the time, that person being Satan. You would recognize him as the Devil. For every good thing the Lord does, like your salvation last night, Satan is right there immediately trying to tear you down. He's all the time trying to get you to stumble and fall out of your walk with the Savior. Before you became a Christian, he did not try to get you to fall because you were already his! Now that you belong to God, Satan wants you back. It's our job to make sure you don't want to go back. Do you understand all that?" Nancy was trying not to sound like a preacher, more like a wife and most of all a friend. They were still walking but now they were arm-in-arm, her head resting on his right shoulder.

"Sure, honey, that makes complete sense. I trust a God and His Son whom I can neither see nor hear but I **CAN** feel His presence in my life. I feel like a thousand pound weight has been lifted off from my shoulders!

Several minutes passed as they walked, arm-in-arm, just enjoying each other's company. Neither of them spoke nor smiled. Harvey never took his eyes from the ocean, Nancy watched closely the other people on the beach. The longer they walked, the more crowded the beach became, both with people and with automobiles. Nancy slowly fixed her gaze on her husband, Harvey never realizing that her head had shifted. Nancy quietly looked at her husband, noticing how much he had changed already. She noticed that she was falling in love with this seemingly new man she was with. As the two walked on the beach she closed her eyes and silently prayed.

"Lord, Jesus, the song that we sing in church comes to mind, 'What an awesome God we serve!' You are truly an awesome God. My husband has changed so much in such a short time. I pray that he will continue to grow, continue his walk in you, and continue to become close to you. Lord, it's true what you say in your Word, that those who remain faithful and trusting will have their prayers answered, but it will be in Your timing and not my timing! Father, I feel selfish asking for more when you have already given me so much, but if it is your will I would like to see Harvey happy in his work and not stressed out like he has been lately. If it is your will, Lord let the sale of the business come through. Let him realize there are other things that he could do...."

"Nan, take a look at that huge yacht heading out the inlet!" Harvey did not know that his wife was praying. "I'd give about anything to be able to do that. I haven't been on a big yacht like that in years, probably not since I was growing up." Harvey's grin stretched from one ear to the other. "Nan, what would you think about leaving O'burg?" They had stopped walking now. Harvey was holding his wife, her head in his hands, looking straight into her eyes. Nancy briefly closed her eyes and again silently prayed. "Lord, you work quick! Please let this come through, but only if it is your will. I want Harvey happy again." She opened her eyes and looked up at him. "How would you ever live without your business? How about your big house?" He put his index finger to her lips, then removed his finger and replaced it with a passionate kiss, just as a wave came crashing in around their feet. Nancy pulled away to look at him, to notice his eyes gazing into hers, to notice the smile crossing his lips. They both looked down at their wet feet, then at the onslaught of surf coming in around their feet. "Honey, this looks like a scene out of a movie or maybe a romance novel." Harvey softened, then hung his head, turned around and faced the ocean, trying hard to hide the emotion that was suddenly overcoming him. He failed miserably. Harvey buried his face in his own hands and cried. Nancy moved around to the other side of him, the waves now coming in around their knees. "Honey, what on earth did I say? Whatever it was I am truly sorry." Harvey was managing to regain control of himself, the events of the last couple days still catching up with him.

"Nancy, these feelings I'm having are all new and different to me. They are good feelings, just different. When you mentioned the movie and the romance novel I came to a sick realization that I have not even taken time to take you to the movies, or sit down with a good book with you next to me. I think I'm realizing all of this walking on the beach with you this morning. I think from now on, we should make time for each other on a daily basis. I think we should do that thing that you do every day together, but I can't think of what you call it!" They were both laughing like a couple of kids

"You must mean my quiet time! Honey, that would be wonderful if we could do that together. It would be a fabulous way to start a new life together. But if we are going to start a new life together, we need to get away from this in-coming tide or we will not have to worry about it. That last wave got about to our waist, so maybe we should think about walking back to the motel and changing before breakfast."

As they were walking back, she turned to look at him. "Harvey, you never answered my question."

"What question was that, Hon?" They kept walking, never missing stride, feet still soaked, still occasionally up to their knees in water.

"Remember, I asked you what you would do without your business and your big house? What about the cars, you know the old Oldsmobile still sitting in the garage. Don't forget your golf outings, and the business deals. Remember?"

"Yeah, I remember. But, after last night, accepting Jesus Christ as personal savior and all that has happened in the last several hours, all that stuff just doesn't seem to matter anymore, but I guess we'll cross that bridge when we come to it."

"Yeah, Honey, that one and a lot more bridges. Only this time we will cross them together, as a single unit." They stopped walking, looked into each other's eyes and passionately kissed again, two kids frolicking in the waves, no longer having a care in the world.